YOUNG READERS' EDITION

NO SURRENDER

A FATHER, A SON, AND AN
EXTRAORDINARY ACT OF HEROISM

CHRIS EDMONDS and
DOUGLAS CENTURY

with WINIFRED CONKLING

HARPER

An Imprint of HarperCollinsPublishers

To my dad, Roddie, his twelve grandchildren and great-grandchildren—Alicia, Kristen, Lauren, Austin, Haylee, Lilly, Hagen, Maylee, Holden, Mollee, Ruthie, Roderick—and future generations around the world.

May they follow the path my dad took.

Library of Congress Control Number: 2019944315
ISBN 978-0-06-296617-9

Typography by David DeWitt
19 20 21 22 23 PC/LSCH 10 9 8 7 6 5 4 3 2 1
❖

First Edition

CONTENTS

PART ONE

PUTTING THE PIECES TOGETHER

1
SHADOWS

Three hours before dawn on Thanksgiving Day 2005, I startled from a peaceful sleep. I was sweating, murmuring the words of my late father, Roddie, which flooded my mind with confusion. I had been dreaming about his World War II journals, neatly written in pencil script. "No one can realize the horrors the infantry soldier goes through," he wrote. "You get scared and I mean scared. Don't let anyone tell you that he wasn't scared."

Those words surprised me. I had never seen my dad afraid of anything. He was fearless; he had a quiet faith in God that made him seem invincible. Dad always marched to the beat of faith, hope, and love. But never fear. Not once in all the years I knew him.

What could have happened to make Dad so afraid?

My dad had served in the infantry in Europe during World War II. He hit the beaches of France several months after the initial D-Day landings, slogged through freezing rain and mud in the fall of 1944, and fought in the icy forests of Belgium during the brutal Battle of the Bulge, the last major German offensive on the Western Front. He spent the final months of the war as a POW—a prisoner of war—in Ziegenhain, a tiny town in central Germany.

I didn't know much more about Dad's service during World War II. Like a lot of members of the Greatest Generation, he never discussed the grisly details of the war. Almost everything I knew I had learned from history books.

Now wide awake, I sat up in bed thinking about Dad. It was a chilly morning in Maryville, Tennessee. The temperature was slightly below freezing. I looked at my wife, Regina, who was still asleep beside me, just as she had been every night for the past twenty-eight years. I pulled the comforter over her shoulder to protect her against the chill.

I went to the bathroom and splashed cold water on my face. I stared into the mirror and asked myself: *Why didn't I ask Dad more questions about the war before he died?*

I had been thinking about my father's wartime experiences since the previous evening. Just after dinner, my daughter Lauren had arrived home from Maryville College, where she and her identical twin sister, Kristen, were earning their degrees in education. Lauren was excited to tell us about her new history project; her group was to prepare an oral history of a family member who had led a noteworthy life.

"Dad, when I told my group that Papaw was a POW in World War II, they said he was *definitely* the story, even though he's no longer alive," Lauren said. "What do you think?"

I told Lauren that I thought it was a great idea. "If I were you, I'd begin with his wartime journals," I said. "Nana has them tucked away somewhere in her house." I told her I had read them several times, but her papaw never talked about the war.

"Not even to Nana?"

"No, not even to Nana."

Later, I thought about Lauren's newfound excitement about her grandfather. Lauren was born in 1985, six months before her papaw Roddie died. She didn't know much about him.

"Two peas in a pod," Dad had said when the twins were born. "I can't tell 'em apart. And they're joining our third li'l pea, big sister, Alicia Marie."

My three girls were inseparable as they grew up in the '80s and '90s. They excelled at school, played house, and collected Barbies. When they were a bit older, they became athletes, taking up cheerleading, gymnastics, softball, basketball, and volleyball. On Friday nights they gathered to watch sitcoms. Papaw Roddie was right: They were "three peas in a pod."

Dad had always seemed to be right about people. He had

an uncanny ability to read a person's heart and see their true character. This served him well all his life. On weekends, Dad used to visit homeless shelters, churches, nursing homes, and veterans' groups in Knoxville, offering encouragement to people in danger of losing hope. He did this simply because he thought it was the right thing to do.

I wanted to help Lauren learn about her papaw and his experiences during World War II, but I knew only the broad strokes of Dad's wartime experiences. I knew he had served as a master sergeant in the US Army. I knew he had fought with the 422nd Regiment of the 106th Infantry Division—the Golden Lions. I knew he had been a prisoner of war, captured sometime during the Battle of the Bulge. But that's all I knew. I was ashamed I didn't know more, that I hadn't asked him more questions when I had the chance. I wished my girls had known my dad.

I had been in my midtwenties, an unemployed father of three, when Dad passed away at the age of sixty-five. He died from congestive heart failure at his Knoxville home on August 8, 1985, twelve days before his sixty-sixth birthday. He chose to die at home, on his own terms. When he learned that he was sick, he checked himself out of the hospital, determined to enjoy his last few months at home.

I don't know how long I had been lost in thought that night as I stood in the kitchen when Regina came to me and asked me what was wrong.

"I feel like I'm letting Lauren—and her sisters—down," I said. "I should know more about Dad's experiences in the war, but I don't." Had I not cared enough to ask him? I didn't know much about his childhood during the Depression or what he was like in high school either. "It was like Dad lived an entire lifetime before I was born."

Regina, who had always loved my dad, listened, then reminded me that he never really talked about his past. "He just lived in the present. That was Roddie. He was a wonderful dad and a wonderful person. A terrific grandfather too."

I thought about what I had read in my father's journal: "If a man lives through a major engagement, he isn't much good after that."

That didn't make sense. My father *was* good after that. "I don't know all that he went through over there, but he didn't seem to have had any aftereffects from the war," I said to Regina.

My father was always optimistic, always upbeat. He used to tell me, "Son, life may knock you down, but you can always fly high as a kite." He wouldn't let things keep him down. He inspired me with his positive outlook. He never quit.

It sounds corny, but Dad was always my hero. Not because he'd survived the Depression and was a member of the Greatest Generation. Not because he served as an infantryman who fought in Europe to save the world from fascism. Not because he stayed in the Army National Guard, and five years later—at the age of thirty—found himself on the front lines again, this time in Korea.

No, Dad was a hero because he was there for me in the ordinary ways. He coached my Little League team, teaching me and my buddies how to lay down a perfect bunt, how to read the opposing pitcher's windup, and how to know when it was safe to steal second base.

He was sincere in his faith too. His love for God and other people was infectious, a model for living that I still try to follow. Dad cared about everyone he met; it didn't matter who they were. He always closed our family prayers with a simple request: "Lord, help us help others who can't help themselves."

Dad was smart, although he never attended college. I never asked why he didn't take advantage of the GI Bill, which would have paid for his education after the war. He was well-read, artistic, and witty, loved wordplay, and was masterful with crossword puzzles.

Thinking about my childhood, I recalled how my older brother, Mike, and some of our buddies from the neighborhood would reenact battles, playing army. I dressed up in Dad's US Army shirt, complete with the master sergeant's gold chevrons above three inverted "rockers" on the shoulder. The shirt was so large that when I ran, the shirttail flapped down to my knees. We would chase each other through the neighborhood pretending we were in the thick of the Battle of the Bulge in the winter of 1944.

My father—five foot five, stout and strong, with a thick head of wavy, sandy hair—loved chewing on a Dutch Masters Corona De Luxe cigar after dinner. He picked up the habit during his military service, but after the war he rarely smoked them; he just clenched them lightly between his teeth. He could make one soggy-tipped Dutch Master last for days.

"Son," he told me once, "these are my 'seegars'—'cause I like to 'see' how long I can make 'em last."

He had a quick wit. When I was fifteen, some friends and I sang at our church's annual Valentine's Day banquet. It was around the time when *American Graffiti* came out, and there was a '50s music revival. My friends and I decided to perform some doo-wop classics. We called ourselves Big Daddy Clive and the Swingin' Five. I sang lead on the Earls' song "Remember Then." As my background singers bobbed and sang in four-part harmony, I jumped onstage wearing a pair of Dad's dressiest shoes, so oversized that I had to stuff the toes with newspaper just to keep them from sliding off my feet. Without missing a beat, Dad jumped up from his front-row seat, pointed his finger at the stage, and shouted, "*There're* my white shoes! I wanted to wear them tonight and wondered where they ran off to!" The audience erupted with laughter and cheers.

Dad had that effect on people. Everybody loved Roddie. Since the war he had been a salesman. Now in his fifties, he was a sales manager who sold prefab modular homes. Throughout Knoxville he was known for being scrupulously fair. He'd seal a deal with a handshake. He was honest, hardworking, and cared about his customers. "I want to see Roddie," prospective buyers would say. Past customers would tell their friends who were looking for a modular home, "Just go see Roddie—he'll treat you right." Roddie—Dad—was what other folks called a "square shooter."

I continued to think about his war journals. Later that night, we went to my mother's house a few miles away. I told her about Lauren's class project and asked about Dad's journals.

My mom, Mary Ann, disappeared into her bedroom. In a dresser drawer was an old cigar box that contained important papers, such as Dad's death certificate, his military discharge papers, expired passport, and life insurance policy. These official papers documented the details of a person's life, but they could never tell the full story. I only knew the story of the last twenty-seven years of Dad's life. I knew Dad and Mom were married in 1953 after he returned from the Korean War, but there was much more to learn. There's always more to learn.

At the bottom of the cigar box, under the other papers,

were two fragile, nearly forgotten journals from 1944 and 1945. They were the size of paperback books, narrow and light enough for an infantryman to tuck into his pocket. The cardboard covers were faded blue, and the pages inside were brittle and yellowed. Holding his journals in my hands, I felt blessed to have been born to good people who worked hard, loved their family, helped their neighbors, served their community, and honored God. But I was burdened too. I felt a responsibility to myself and my family to know what happened to Dad during the war.

For her project, Lauren read the journals, combing through the delicate pages for details to use in her presentation. Regina and I listened as she read aloud from her papaw's past: "A lot of things I am not going to write," Roddie had confided in his journal. "Because they aren't exactly nice to talk about. I know God was with us, and he answered our prayers. I learned men, even better than before. Some were good, some were bad, some were better, and some were worse."

As Lauren read aloud, we all began to tear up. I realized this was the closest my daughter was ever going to get to her papaw, reading a few lines he had written down sixty years before, in the winter of 1945, twelve years before I was born and decades before Lauren came into our lives.

She traced her finger on another line. "'I will not tell anyone the true happenings—by true, I mean some of the worst things that happened to us as POWs,'" Lauren read. She looked up at me. "Did Papaw ever describe his experiences to you?"

"No, I asked Dad about it when I was your age. All he said was 'Son, we were humiliated.' I asked a bunch of times, but that's all he'd ever say. That one word, 'humiliated.'"

Lauren shook her head and said, "I can't imagine what Papaw had to go through." None of us could.

I sat down to read through my father's journals cover to cover. I hadn't looked through them in decades. It felt as if I were walking through an old house, with hallways leading to new secrets. In those wartime journals I could *hear* Dad's voice, just like he was sitting at the table with me. But there was so much I did not know. And there wasn't enough written to unlock his past.

The last time I had read the journals I was in college. Now I was a middle-aged man, a grandfather, an ordained minister, still trying to make sense of the words my dad wrote when he was twenty-five years old. Lauren's school project had lit a fire inside me. As I read through the journals again and again, Dad's mysterious words hit me with new meaning. I had forgotten, but there were even illustrations, floor plans, and menus for a restaurant called the Jolly Chef that the starving POWs probably fantasized about opening after the war.

There were names and addresses of some of the men who survived the POW camp with Dad, including:

ARTHUR LEVITT—BRONX, NEW YORK

EMANUEL FRAWERT—PATERSON, NEW JERSEY

MORRIS CHESTER—BALTIMORE, MARYLAND

SYDNEY S. FRIEDMAN—SHAKER HEIGHTS, OHIO

JOHN V. SELG—BROOKLYN, NEW YORK

CARL E. JOHNSON—GRAND RAPIDS, MICHIGAN

WARD R. RICHARDSON—LUDINGTON, MICHIGAN

EDWARD W. BERRY—GRAND RAPIDS, MICHIGAN

RALPH H. WAHLMAN—WILLISVILLE, ILLINOIS

CARL FALCH—MIAMIVILLE, OHIO

HENRY E. FREEDMAN—DORCHESTER, MASSACHUSETTS

PAUL STERN—BRONX, NEW YORK

These eighteen- and nineteen-year-old boys had come from every part of the country, from different backgrounds and cultures, to fight together for a common cause. Their names, each written in his own hand, added to my sense of mystery.

Dad wrote briefly about the ferocious battles, the courage of his "boys," a few details about their capture and the harsh conditions at the Nazi camps. His descriptions were short—brief facts, fragmented sentences, mental notes, personal shorthand, words scribbled in haste.

Dad's war had ended several decades ago. I was sure he had seen enough horrors to haunt a lifetime. What happened to him? How did he cope?

I couldn't escape the fact that, despite the horrors hinted at in their pages, Dad's journals had been written with fierce faith in God and hopes of something bigger and better on the horizon.

Lord, I don't know what happened over there, but you do, I prayed. *Please help me find out.*

2
THE BEGINNING

I slowly began digging into my dad's military service, but months flew by before I made much progress. Then, in February 2009, I sat down at my computer and googled "Master Sergeant Roddie Edmonds."

I expected to be directed to a World War II National Archives database or the 106th Infantry Division veterans' page, but the first link that popped up was an article in the *New York Times* from July 30, 2008, titled "Richard Nixon's Search for a New York Home." The story recounted how the disgraced former president had tried to buy an apartment in Manhattan. No one would sell to him following his resignation from the White House, and no one wanted the former president to be their neighbor.

According to the story, Lester Tanner, a prominent Harvard-educated attorney, eventually stepped up. He had been a lifelong Democrat, friends with Bobby Kennedy, and was elected as a Kennedy delegate during the 1968 presidential campaign. Lester disagreed with Nixon's politics, but he was appalled by the hatred of New York City residents. He decided the right thing to do was to sell Nixon his twelve-room town house in the middle of Manhattan.

I wasn't sure what this story had to do with my dad.

I kept reading, and Lester mentioned that during World War II, he had been held in a Nazi prisoner-of-war camp near Ziegenhain, Germany. He said that his "brave officer," Master Sergeant Roddie Edmonds, had defied the camp's commander, saving Lester's life, until they could be liberated by US troops.

I was stunned.

My dad was a master sergeant. His name had been spelled correctly. He had been held in Ziegenhain. The man in the article had to be Dad, but I didn't know anything about him saving a life in a POW camp.

I showed the article to my wife, Regina, waiting for her to tell me I had misread something.

"I can't believe it," she finally said. "It's got to be Roddie."

We were left with more questions. Who was Lester Tanner? Was he still alive? What did he know about Dad?

I scrolled down to the comment section. I wasn't sure who to write to: The story's author? Lester Tanner? Instead, I wrote to Dad.

Thank you, Dad, for doing what was right and for living out your values. Your heroic actions continue to touch our lives. A proud son. —Chris Edmonds

Over the next few weeks, I dug into Dad's journals, looking for a clue that could help answer my questions.

Most of Dad's entries were clear and specific, but others made little sense. Reading them was both exhilarating and frustrating: the more I studied the journals, the less I seemed to know. I needed Dad to help me solve the puzzle.

What was really driving me crazy were the missing pages. It looked as if Dad had ripped out a few pages, right in the middle of one of the books. Dad's story ended midsentence.

I enjoyed my last hot meal on the evening of the 17th, because the morning of

And then nothing. Just blank pages. No finished thought. No indentations pressed into the blank pages from a heavy pencil. Nothing but more mystery and even more questions.

Where were the missing pages? Had Dad intentionally removed or destroyed them? Why?

On the page following the blank ones, the journal continued with no connection to his previous thoughts.

I guess the reason I am writing this, mainly is to relieve my mind, and while some of the events are fresh in my mind.

There was a series of blank pages, and then he started writing again at the back of the journal. Maybe the mystery lay in the pages he hadn't touched, the empty pages he'd left without a mark? Why would he have left so many empty pages? Had it been to fool the Germans if they found the notebook? Or had things become so bad that he hadn't had the will or strength to write?

Then there were the last two pages with nothing more than cryptic notes, scribbled in haste:

Army career

Capture

First night and the long march

Gerolstein

Trip to Bad Orb

Jewish moved out

Hiding

And there was a mysterious phrase that ended abruptly with his pencil trailing off into indistinguishable markings:

Before the commander . . .

I didn't know what any of it meant. I wished Dad were here to explain. I wish I had been more interested in Dad's life and less in my own.

Then I saw it. Right there, a few pages into the POW signatures:

Lester J. Tannenbaum

1384 Grand Concourse

Bronx, N.Y.

Lester Tannenbaum. Although the last names differed, that *had* to be the same Lester Tanner from the *New York Times.*

He must have changed his name after the war. He had been in my dad's journal the entire time, along with the address of where he had lived before the war. I wondered if Lester or any of the other men listed in the journal were still alive and had stories to share that would help me better understand my dad.

Finding Lester and learning more about my father was important, but I let life distract me until one evening I was watching the news with Regina and a report mentioned that nearly three hundred veterans of World War II died each day.

I was shocked. I worried that I had missed my chance to find Mr. Tanner. I had no idea, but Lester had started looking for me after reading the comment I had left on the *New York Times* website. He found my contact information online and sent me an email with a short note of introduction and his phone number. My prayers were answered.

I called the number. I was nervous and really didn't know what to say, but I was excited to talk to Lester. The phone rang and rang, then rolled over to voice mail. Disappointed, I left a detailed message and promised to call back.

A few days later, I saw that Lester had called and left a message. I called him back, thrilled to finally connect with a man from the Greatest Generation, a man who knew some of the mysteries of my father's life. I felt a mysterious bond with him over something that had happened nearly seventy years ago.

We started out with small talk, mostly about our work, our families, and our grandchildren. It was hard for him to hear me on the phone, so at Lester's suggestion, I agreed to email him.

While Lester had a difficult time hearing me, I heard him loud and clear. He said he was awed by Dad's bravery and eternally grateful for actions that helped save his life— *and* the lives of others.

Dad saved *other* men too? At that point I sensed that my father's story might be bigger than I had imagined.

3
WONDERLAND

I wanted to meet Lester, so I asked if Regina, Austin (our ten-year-old grandson), and I could visit him. He was happy to have us, so we made plans. Other than Dad, no one in my family had ever been to New York City. It was exciting. We were preparing for a trip to the Big Apple to meet a soldier from my father's generation. Lester Tanner was a respected attorney who might tell me things about my father I didn't know and help me unravel the mystery of Dad's time as a POW.

"My wife, Regina, doesn't like to fly," I said, explaining that we planned to drive to New York. I asked Lester if he could suggest a place for us to stay.

"Might I suggest the Harvard Club?" he asked.

"Can I get a room at the Harvard Club?"

"No," he said, "but I can."

I was nervous about the expense. "How much is that

going to cost per night?" I asked.

"For you, nothing," Lester said. "It's the least I can do for the son of the man who saved my life. I owe *everything* to your father."

This wasn't the response I expected from a man I barely knew.

We drove up from Tennessee, stopping overnight in Winchester, Virginia. When we approached New York City, we had to drive in stop-and-go traffic, *under* the Hudson River. In the Lincoln Tunnel, my GPS lost service. I was driving way too slow for city traffic, so other drivers were honking and cursing at me. I ended up in the wrong lane, and a moment later we spilled out onto the streets of Manhattan, utterly lost and in a bit of panic. But somehow, we made it to the Harvard Club on West Forty-Fourth Street.

The halls of the Harvard Club were covered in plush crimson carpet; the walls in high-gloss crimson paint. Portraits of Harvard graduates reminded me of a who's who of US history: Presidents Teddy Roosevelt, Franklin Roosevelt, John F. Kennedy, and Barack Obama. There were also portraits of Supreme Court justices, playwrights, novelists, Nobel Laureates, movie stars, and war heroes. In addition to paintings, there were stuffed animals—immense swordfish and sailfish, the heads of moose and antelope, and, in the cavernous main hall, a majestic Asian elephant with three-foot-long tusks.

The day finally came for me to meet Lester. I anxiously waited for him in the lobby of the Harvard Club. I assumed I was looking for a stooped older man with horn-rimmed glasses and a cane. I was surprised when I was greeted by a powerfully built older man of six feet, with a head of thick, swept-back warm brown hair, wearing an elegant blue business suit, starched white shirt, and a yellow silk tie in a perfect Windsor knot.

"You must be Chris," Lester said. "You resemble your father."

We shook hands warmly. I was surprised by the strength of Lester's grip. I tried to imagine how Lester must have looked in 1944, a young soldier serving alongside my father. Lester alone knew things about him that I could not possibly imagine. Lester, like Dad, seemed so normal and well-adjusted. For a moment I paused and held Lester's hand, in awe of him, Dad, and all who had served so well.

Lester guided me upstairs to the library. "We can speak in private," he said. "And it will be much easier for me to hear than in the noisy dining room."

Even in the quiet of the library, Lester had difficulty hearing. He scooted his chair right next to me, leaning in so close I could feel his warm breath against my cheek.

"Your father was cut from a different cloth than the rest of us," Lester said. "He was never arrogant and disrespectful.

His style was simply to make us proud of what we were being called upon to do in defense of the republic. We knew he respected us and was devoted to our survival in combat. He never left any doubt that he was in command. He expected every one of his orders to be followed."

I shook my head in surprise. "Growing up, my dad was such a soft-spoken, fun-loving guy," I said. "It's hard for me to imagine Dad ordering other men around."

"Your father led by example," Lester said. "He taught his men to keep their rifles clean, to develop their skills on the firing range, and to fix their bayonets to defend themselves in close quarters. Many of the men in his regiment were young, barely out of high school. Roddie's experience and knowledge gave us all confidence," Lester continued. "Your father was of a different generation, Chris. We called him 'The Old Man.'"

The Old Man? "Lester," I said. "My dad was barely *four* years older than you!"

Lester was shocked. "Four years?" he asked. "I assumed he was at least thirty. His knowledge and conduct as the chief enlisted man in a regiment of five thousand soldiers enhanced that image of maturity. Chris, that's astonishing."

We sat for a moment in silence. "Lester, I know it must be hard for you to talk about," I said. "But what exactly happened in that German POW camp? What did my dad do at Ziegenhain?"

"What your father did at Ziegenhain is one of the most remarkable things I've ever witnessed—it is the defining moment of my life. And, Chris, I should tell you, I believe your father is deserving of the Congressional Medal of Honor."

I was speechless. "You think dad is deserving of the highest honor of our military, the Medal of Honor?"

"The Medal of Honor." Lester nodded. "But before I tell you what happened in Germany, please tell me more about your father."

I told Lester what little I knew about Dad's life before I was born. Later that week, I left New York on a mission to find out what happened to him as a prisoner of war and help him be considered for a Medal of Honor.

Since then, I have interviewed other soldiers who had served with my father and Lester. I have conducted research at the Library of Congress and the National Archives. I have read many books about the Battle of the Bulge and other accounts of World War II prisoners of war. Using these voices and stories, I have pieced together the story of my father's life and wartime service. I have a greater appreciation for the man my father was and the struggles he overcame, starting with his childhood during the Great Depression.

PART TWO

MY FATHER'S STORY

4
FAMILY

Roderick Waring (Roddie) Edmonds was born on August 20, 1919, in Knoxville, Tennessee. He was the last of five boys born to Jennie and Thomas Calvin "T.C." Edmonds. The family didn't have many possessions, but they had what they believed mattered most: gratitude for life, respect for others, and a devotion to God and family.

In the weeks after my father was born, Knoxville went through a period of violence and rioting. On August 30, a lynch mob stormed the county jail in search of Maurice Mays, an African American former deputy sheriff who had been accused of murdering a twenty-seven-year-old white woman named Bertie Lindsey. The rioters looted the jail, released the white inmates, and provoked a gun battle with the residents of a predominantly black neighborhood just blocks from my grandparents' home.

The governor called in the Tennessee National Guard.

Before peace was restored, seven people were killed—six black and one white—and scores were injured. Knoxville's race riot was part of a nationwide epidemic of civil unrest, known as the Red Summer. From May to October, violent racial incidents swept cities across the United States, resulting in an estimated six hundred deaths.

In spite of this prejudice—or maybe because of it— Roddie grew up in a home that rejected all forms of intolerance and racial hatred. He was raised to follow the Golden Rule: love everyone as you love yourself.

Roddie experienced tragedy when he was just three years old. On Saturday, June 24, 1922, an unusually hot day, even by Knoxville standards, thirty-nine-year-old Jennie spent the day with her boys. She had recently learned that she was pregnant again. Jennie felt run-down, and she had been hoarse for several days. When she went to bed that night, her throat felt tight.

The following morning, her neck was swollen. She had a cough, which grew worse during the day. As the hours passed, it became increasingly difficult for her to breathe. The following night, she died from complications of a goiter, an enlargement of the thyroid gland caused by an iodine deficiency. Her airway had become blocked, and she died from asphyxiation, or suffocation. Alive one minute, gone the next, along with her unborn baby. It was a great loss for

Roddie and the family. T.C., who never remarried, recorded her death on the front and back leaves of his pocket-sized Bible, which he carried with him the rest of his life.

T.C., a skilled wallpaper hanger, was left to raise the boys alone. His older sister, Sarah Edmonds Hickman—Aunt Sallie—helped raise Roddie. Soon after his mother died, Roddie moved in with Aunt Sallie and her husband, William, a retired carpenter. They lived across the river from the University of Tennessee, and on fall afternoons, he could sometimes hear whistles and shouts from the fields where the Tennessee Volunteers football team practiced. Roddie loved playing baseball and football with his neighborhood friends on top of the hill at Fort Dickerson. The houses on his street had wide front porches, where families relaxed on swings or napped in rocking chairs while the kids rode pedal cars or made fast getaways on their bikes. The neighborhood was a broad extended family. Everyone looked out for each other.

Roddie cared for others, even when he was a young boy. In December 1926, he wrote a letter to Santa Claus, which was published in the evening edition of the Knoxville paper.

I am a little boy 7 years old. I go to school all I can and want you to bring me a car big enough to ride in, a black board, a derrick, lots of nuts of all kinds, and plenty of candy. Please dear Santa bring Boots something nice too. He is a little sick

boy who lives with us and he needs an invalid's chair. Don't
forget us, we are good little boys. I am a little boy without a
mother and Boots is without a father.
Roderick Edmonds.
702 Peddie St.

When Roddie was ten, the Great Depression hit Knoxville.
Following the stock market crash of 1929, his father had
trouble finding work. Some families left town and returned
to the farms, where they could grow their own food. Others
depended on soup kitchens. Families could no longer pay
for telephones and other services; many could not afford to
buy all the food they needed. In the winter of 1932, Roddie
and his family experienced severe hunger for the first time.
Instead of complaining, Roddie learned to appreciate all he
had, a practice he continued throughout his life.

In the presidential campaign of 1930, New York governor
Franklin Delano Roosevelt promised the nation a "New
Deal." President Roosevelt, recognizing the crisis in the
rural South, signed the Tennessee Valley Authority Act
in May 1933. People living in Tennessee needed help. The
average income was less than $640 per year; malaria was
common; eroded and depleted soil had led to crop failures;
and Tennessee's best timber had long ago been cut.

The Tennessee Valley Authority transformed the region.

It put thousands of unemployed men to work building dams and other projects. It brought electricity to new parts of the state, energizing industry and helping to make farms more productive. By the fall of 1933, the fourth year of the Depression, Roddie was an eighth grader at Boyd Junior High. While many older students had to quit school to work or help with the family farm, Roddie was able to stay in school.

Roddie excelled at his studies; his favorite subject was history. He learned how the past had a powerful influence on the present, and how it could influence future events. He didn't have many material things, but he lived in a good home, sang in his church choir, and loved baseball.

As a young teenager, Roddie's life changed when he became a Christian. He described the experience as being "saved" and experiencing "believer's peace," which he noted in the back of his Bible with three verses: Romans 3:23; Romans 6:23; and Romans 10:9–10.

From that day forward, his life was different. He wanted to serve God *and* people. He did not forget the moment he found his faith, even during those dark and desperate days he was held as a prisoner of war during World War II.

In the fall of 1935, Roddie began the tenth grade, his first year at Knoxville High School. He joined the school's nationally recognized Junior Reserve Officer Training

Corps (JROTC) team and became proficient with firearms. Every day he would walk almost two and a half miles to school, many days in his JROTC uniform, with only one hard biscuit for his lunch. Roddie graduated from high school in June 1938 and got a job working as a stock clerk at the wallpaper company where his father was a paper hanger. He was fortunate to find work, because Knoxville was still at the tail end of the Depression. He was dating his high school sweetheart, Marie Solomon, a girl from the neighborhood.

In March 1941, nine months before the Japanese attacked Pearl Harbor and the United States joined the war, Roddie enlisted in the US Army. He was sent as a private to Fort Jackson, an infantry training base in South Carolina.

During his induction process, he and the other enlistees were handed a neatly typed introduction to military life. "You are now on your way toward the Induction Station where you will very shortly join the greatest 'team' in the world," the paper read, in part. "Whatever may have been your *personal* reasons for volunteering, the wearing of the uniform will make you a member of the best team of other men like yourself who seek to preserve the American way of life."

Roddie was twenty-one years old.

5
SOLDIER

Standing with other recruits, my father raised his right hand, pledged his allegiance to the United States, and swore that he would "support and defend the Constitution of the United States against all enemies, foreign and domestic . . . according to regulations and the Uniform Code of Military Justice. So help me God."

At the time of his enlistment, Roddie was part of a massive ramp-up in the US Armed Forces. New divisions were being created almost weekly as hundreds of thousands of new soldiers registered for service.

Following his swearing-in, Roddie found himself standing naked in a long line as an assembly line of physicians examined every part of his body. He stood five feet, five inches tall and weighed 143 pounds.

A nervous recruit standing near Roddie asked a doctor if he thought he would pass the physical.

"Soldier," the doctor replied, "you're already in the army."

Roddie, now Private Edmonds, was assigned to Headquarters Company of the 121st Regiment, Thirtieth Infantry Division. He was part of the Gray Bonnets, a hard-nosed infantry regiment of the Georgia National Guard commanded by Captain Charles R. Irwin. President Franklin D. Roosevelt and the Congress had ordered the National Guard into service on August 31, 1940. The Germans nicknamed this division "Roosevelt's SS" because of their toughness in combat.

First stop was a thirteen-week basic training program. Every day was like the one before: up for roll call at 6:30 a.m., train all day, breaking only for meals, then back to bed, exhausted. For Roddie, the South Carolina heat and humidity were draining. The pouring rain pelted the men's helmets and drenched their drab olive-colored uniforms, weighing down their gear. The men trained in all kinds of conditions, even during thunderstorms, hurricanes, and the occasional tornado that brought damaging winds, torrential downpours, and hail the size of golf balls. When the soldiers complained, their sergeant reminded them that bad weather would be the least of their troubles in battle.

Roddie and his buddies marched daily—thirty-two-mile endurance marches, two-hour speed marches, and two-mile "double time" sprints. Roddie competed against other infantry privates in the one-hundred-yard speed obstacle course, which required the men to run in full combat gear. The men jumped over a two-foot hurdle, vaulted a four-foot fence, ran a maze of posts and lintels, climbed a seven-foot wall, jumped a six-foot-wide ditch, and crossed a high beam. In another obstacle course, they rope-climbed a twelve-foot wall, sprinted up a tilted ladder and across a log, jumped between a framework of planks, swung and monkey-barred over a water-filled ditch, and then crawled through a narrow tunnel and under a wire entanglement. Completing the course felt like an accomplishment. The repetitive drills and calisthenics, coupled with the countless push-ups and pull-ups, was the hottest and most grueling experience of his life. But after only a few weeks of boot camp, he felt himself getting stronger.

Roddie's training also included intensive study in courses such as Army Organization, Military Discipline, Articles of War, Hygiene, First Aid, Combat Intelligence, Weapons, Mines and Booby Traps, and Close Combat. As part of his education and training, he was exposed to nonlethal agents like phenacyl chloride—tear gas—and taught to rapidly slip on his gas mask. The training he feared most was the "infiltration" course. While machine guns fired live rounds over his head, he had to crawl fifty yards under barbed wire. The exercise was meant to simulate battle, but nothing could prepare them for the horrors they would face as soldiers in combat.

Roddie never stopped training. He distinguished himself on the shooting range as a sharpshooter. His rifle skill, honed during his hours of practice in the JROTC program, earned him the highest classification of rifle expert. He could handle any caliber of military firearms, but his specialty was the M1 carbine, the lightweight .30-caliber semiautomatic rifle, which he could fire with deadly accuracy.

He also excelled as a leader. His skill with people and his calm, commanding demeanor won him the respect of both his fellow soldiers and his superiors.

At the time Roddie enlisted, the United States was at peace, but the war was raging in England. Ten days after Roddie arrived at Fort Jackson, President Roosevelt came for an unannounced visit to inspect the camp and watch the troops parade. Roosevelt's short visit to Fort Jackson inspired Roddie.

It wasn't the first time Roddie had been impressed by FDR. On September 2, 1940, six months before Roddie had enlisted, the president and Mrs. Roosevelt passed through Knoxville on their way to dedicate the Great Smoky Mountains National Park. Roddie had joined the flag-waving crowd as the presidential motorcade passed.

President Roosevelt's speech had become more urgent and pointed to possible war. Only hours before, two Royal Navy destroyers had been sunk by Nazi U-boats in the North Sea, and more than two hundred German bombers attacked London and other English cities.

"The greatest attack that has ever been launched against individual freedom is nearer the Americas than ever before," President Roosevelt warned. "If we are to survive, we cannot be soft. . . . Squirrel rifles are no longer adequate to defend the nation. We must prepare in a thousand ways."

By the summer of 1941, the American military was gearing up for war. In June, Roddie joined in a large-scale military training with seventy-seven thousand army troops in Tennessee. Heat, hygiene, and shortages of food, water, and fuel were constant concerns, but the soldiers' good humor made these maneuvers manageable. The lack of rainfall made dust an enormous problem during moves and marches. When rain did arrive, the dust became mud. Temperatures hit the upper nineties as Roddie and the other men engaged in their military exercises.

Toughened by the long, brutal marches in full gear, Roddie learned how to hide himself and his equipment from aerial observers and how to move with his unit. Even the exercises were dangerous and deadly: in the first two and a half weeks of combat simulation, six soldiers died, and the death toll reached twelve by the end of the month.

The training helped shape Roddie into a well-rounded soldier, one who had endured prolonged bouts of hunger, extreme thirst, constant fatigue, and the relentless stresses of war. On June 25, when Secretary of War Henry L. Stimson observed the training, Roddie stood out among the enlisted men as a soldier with great promise.

Returning to Fort Jackson, Roddie earned rapid promotions from his commanding officers. By the end of October 1941, after only six months as a private, Roddie was promoted to private first class. Nine months later, in July 1942, he was bumped up to technician fourth grade—radio operator—and, by the end of August 1942, he was promoted to staff sergeant. Finally, on January 19, 1943, Roddie was promoted to master sergeant and communications chief of his regimental company, advancing from recruit to master sergeant in only twenty-two months, a virtually unprecedented achievement. Today it may take fifteen years for someone to make master sergeant, but Roddie achieved the rank by age twenty-two.

"Congratulations," Roddie's commanding officer said. "You're the youngest soldier to make master sergeant."

Everything changed on December 7, 1941, when Japan attacked Pearl Harbor, killing more than 2,400 Americans. Immediately, men of all ages—driven by outrage, anger, and love of country—rushed to enlist in the army, navy, and marines. College students delayed their degrees, workers left their jobs, and teenagers in high school too young to enlist lined up to lie about their age and join anyway.

Veterans of World War I and old men who had never served in the military tried to join the armed forces. Within days, the ranks of the military swelled by tens of thousands. Total strangers from across the country bonded as one to preserve freedom.

For Roddie, the attack on Pearl Harbor was personal. His brother Robert was serving at the Pearl Harbor Naval Station. Roddie waited nervously for news of his brother's condition; finally, after several days, the family learned that Robert had survived the attack without injury. On December 11, 1941—four days after the United States declared war on Japan—Adolf Hitler declared war against the United States. Eventually, sixty-one countries would join the global fight that became known as World War II.

In mid-1942, seven months after the attack on Pearl Harbor, British prime minister Winston Churchill secretly traveled to Fort Jackson to visit the troops. Roddie and the other soldiers were inspired by the charismatic visitor from England, while Churchill, weary from war, found renewed strength and optimism from the strength of the US infantry.

In November 1942, Roddie slipped away to Knoxville on a weekend pass. That Saturday night, in an intimate ceremony of family and friends, Roddie married his girlfriend, Marie Solomon, a petite local beauty from his neighborhood. Marie was three years younger than Roddie. She had worked as a clerk at the Vestal Lumber Manufacturing Company since she graduated from Knoxville High in 1941. Roddie was looking forward to post-army life back in Knoxville, but he knew his country needed him first.

6
LEADER

On March 15, 1943, the 106th Infantry Division was activated in response to the need for more land forces in preparation for the eventual invasion of Europe. The 106th Division—the last infantry division created during World War II—adopted the motto: "To make history is our aim."

Roddie and eighteen hundred other men from his previous division were transferred into the 106th. They were known as the Golden Lions. The divisional insignia was a yellow lion's face on a bright blue background encircled by white and red borders. The blue represented the infantry, the red stood for the artillery, and the lion's face was symbolic of strength and courage.

Roddie was thrilled to be in a new division in charge of men ready to fight Hitler. On March 29, 1943, their training began. Roddie was a master sergeant, tasked as communications chief in Headquarters Company of the 422nd

Regiment. He was responsible for installing and operating wire, radio, and air-to-ground communications, as well as directing transmission and receipt of calls or messages. His most important task was instructing and training his men in the techniques of field communication. On the battlefield, communication was of life-or-death importance.

He was also tasked with the physical transformation and education of the division's new men. When he wasn't running them ragged, Roddie also made sure to teach his men to know and respect their rifle. Most of the infantrymen carried the M1 Garand .30-06 caliber, the workhorse rifle of World War II; Roddie still preferred the M1 carbine he'd mastered during his infantry training. By putting his men through drill after drill, Roddie had them so familiar with the Garand that they could fieldstrip and reassemble their rifles while blindfolded.

One of Roddie's new young recruits was Lester J. Tannenbaum. Lester was born in the Bronx, New York, on August 8, 1923. His father, Louis, had emigrated from Austria in 1911 at age fourteen. He didn't have a formal education, but he learned English and read the *New York Times* every day. "On Sunday the whole family would gather in the living room and the *Times* would be spread out," Lester said. "Everyone would read a section." Louis ran a small tailoring business on the Lower East Side. The Bronx was a thriving community for immigrant Jews. In 1930, nearly 50 percent of the borough was Jewish.

The Tannenbaum family kept Orthodox traditions. The family kept a kosher home, and Lester had his bar mitzvah at age thirteen. During the Great Depression, the family struggled but stayed together. "I was six years old in 1929 when the Depression started," Lester said. "And I was seventeen years old in 1940 when it ended." His father was a businessman; he had a contract to make uniforms for the policemen and firemen of New York City. He had enough money coming in that the family was secure; they never went hungry.

Lester was an exceptionally bright student, who entered high school at age twelve. "At that time the only elite high school in New York was Townsend Harris," he said. Lester was one of one hundred students accepted to the school, based on his scores on a citywide test. "It was a very traditional, classics-based school."

In addition to learning Latin, students were required to study a second, modern language. "I took German because I thought I was going to be a doctor," Lester said. When he was fifteen years old, he enrolled at City College.

Lester started out as a premed student, but he disliked medical studies and switched to pre-law. He registered for military service when he turned eighteen, four months before Pearl Harbor. He was exempt from the draft until he finished college, but he wanted to serve.

Lester's brother, five years his senior, was already in the service—ultimately commissioned as a major with the army's Transportation Corps—and Lester was anxious to complete his coursework as quickly as possible to go for a commission in the US Army Air Forces. His dream was to be a fighter pilot, in the cockpit of a P-51 Mustang or a P-38 Lightning, terrorizing Messerschmitt fighters over the skies of occupied Europe. He accelerated his program and took extra credits so that he could graduate a year early and begin his service.

He was inducted into the army infantry at Fort Dix in New Jersey. "I felt great, couldn't wait," he said. "If anything, I was afraid I wouldn't be able to get into the war. I was nineteen years old. When you're nineteen you think nothing can happen to you."

Despite his preference for being a pilot, he was assigned to Fort Jackson and joined the 422nd Infantry Regiment. Then almost immediately, in March 1943, he was assigned to Headquarters Company of the regiment, where he met Roddie. The regiment had five thousand enlisted men in three battalions. Each battalion had three rifle companies, as well as special companies like the Cannon Company, Tank Company, Heavy Weapons Company, and Supply Company. The regimental headquarters was responsible for directing all these units.

Lester spent the first thirteen weeks of basic training

under Roddie's leadership. "Roddie was my commander and later my close friend," Lester said. "He combined the unusual virtues of courage and sensitivity." As the ranking noncommissioned officer (NCO), Roddie was the right-hand man of the 422nd regimental commander. "Roddie's word carried a lot of weight," Lester said.

Roddie was known for his calm but firm demeanor. He was a tough sergeant, but he was fair. His sole aim was getting the young recruits under his command ready for combat. He taught his men how to load their backpacks so that they could survive in any situation. He accompanied his men on every march, no matter the weather. Most importantly, Roddie taught his men the importance of following orders and respecting the chain of command, because failing to do so could get you killed.

Frank Cerenzia was another young soldier under Roddie's direction. Frank—Frankie—was a charismatic young Italian American from New York who became Roddie's closest confidant. Like Roddie, Frankie was a married man; he had married days before he left for basic training. They understood each other because they both knew how it felt to be married, enlisted, and away from their wives. They also shared a strong faith.

Frankie had been born in Brooklyn on April 23, 1924. He had attended two years of high school before enlisting in the US Army in February 1943. "I gave Frankie his basic training and he was one of my best soldiers," Roddie wrote in his journal. "We became very close and had a lot in common. He's an alright guy, and my best friend—truthful and sincere. I always admire a man who is truthful."

Roddie, Frankie, and Lester became very close at Fort Jackson. Though Roddie outranked them and was clearly in command while on duty, he was relaxed and light-hearted when they were off duty. During their free time, they listened to big band music—Glenn Miller, the Dorsey Brothers, and Benny Goodman, as well as Count Basie, Duke Ellington, Ella Fitzgerald, and Frank Sinatra. But their group was soon split up. Roddie recommended Lester for the infantry school, where he spent three months training to become a noncommissioned officer. After the three months, Lester applied for the US Army Air Forces and trained to be a fighter pilot on the Lockheed P-38 Lightning, a complex twin-engine turbocharged aircraft armed with 20-mm-caliber cannon and four .50-caliber machine guns.

Back at Fort Jackson, Roddie, Frankie, and the rest of the 106th continued with their training. They didn't know when, but they knew the day was coming when they would be called upon to do what they were trained to do—to fight and to make sure that justice and freedom prevailed in the world.

7
SCHOLARS AND SOLDIERS

Back in Cleveland, Ohio, Sydney Friedman was selected as potential army officer material. Sydney—known as "Skip" to his family—was born in Cleveland on April 24, 1924, to Louis and Pearl Friedman, immigrants who'd come from Eastern Europe to the United States in 1922. They settled in Cleveland and opened a dry-cleaning business.

Skip played football and wanted to be a journalist. In high school, he worked for the *Cleveland Press* newspaper. He enrolled at Case Western Reserve University, and when he turned eighteen, Skip and his older brother Morrie enlisted in the army.

"We took basic infantry training at Camp Wheeler, Georgia," Skip said. "It was very tough and rigorous training." Both Skip and his brother were chosen for the Army Specialized Training Program (ASTP), which was sometimes called the largest educational program in the nation's history. Immediately after Pearl Harbor, many colleges and universities faced an uncertain future. Many of their students had enlisted or were on the verge of being drafted. Schools worried about dwindling enrollment, and the army realized that the military might not have enough well-educated officers and technical specialists. Their solution was to send promising students to college and then give them military assignments.

The ASTP targeted the best and brightest from high schools and colleges around the country. Some candidates were as young as sixteen. Eligibility was based solely on intellect and previous educational success. Candidates had to be high school graduates and score a minimum of 110 on the Army General Classification Test, or ten points higher than what was required for Officer Candidates School. Those in the program were under strict military discipline and wore regulation uniforms. They were subject to inspections, marched to classes and meals, and had mandatory lights-out at 10:30 p.m. They were not allowed to participate in any intercollegiate sports.

The country had never before attempted anything like the ASTP. The army was training and educating hundreds of thousands of soldier-scholars on a fast track. All advanced degrees were accelerated: four-year programs were covered in about two years. The program was challenging. Those in the program faced twenty-four hours of classroom and lab instruction, twenty-four hours of study, five hours of military instruction, and six hours of physical instruction each week.

The program was controversial. Some complained about its size and its preferential treatment of certain soldiers. Some in the military thought the program took young men with leadership potential away from combat positions, where they were most needed. Others claimed the army leadership had only supported the program to keep the universities from lobbying Congress and the administration to protest the lowering of the draft age from twenty-one to eighteen. One congressman derided the ASTP as a program "designed to keep the sons of the rich and powerful out of combat," allowing them to "loaf and play" on campuses "while the sons of honest working men perished on the field of battle."

Within the military, soldiers in the ASTP were mocked as geeks, bookworms, and "Quiz Kids." They were easy to spot: ASTP students wore a unique shoulder patch depicting a blue "Lamp of Knowledge" on their uniforms.

Today, the ASTP is regarded as the boldest and most far-reaching educational experiment in American history. The ASTP would leave a profound footprint on US history and the culture of the twentieth century; the program has been called a groundbreaking social experiment in merit-based advancement, one that helped to more fully "democratize American society by selecting its trainees based on their inherent ability rather than on their family's socio-economic status." Notable participants in the program include US senators Bob Dole and Frank Church, US secretary of state Henry Kissinger, New York City mayor Ed Koch, and numerous prominent writers, entertainers, and artists, such as Gore Vidal, Kurt Vonnegut, and Mel Brooks.

As an ASTP student, Skip Friedman found himself in the Deep South, studying engineering at the University of Alabama in Tuscaloosa. In spring 1942, as he was departing for Alabama from Cleveland Union Terminal, Skip met a group of coeds who'd come to "say goodbye to the boys." Among them were two young Jewish women, twins Penny and Ruth Klausner.

"Penny and I formed a quick connection," Skip said. "As we boarded the train, Penny looked up at me with her nice eyes and said, 'We'd like to know what's going on in the army during these wartime days. Why don't you write us and we'll write back?' So I quickly took out my pad and wrote down her address. And we started writing letters. That fateful meeting, our correspondence, and two dates before I shipped overseas sustained me through the terrors and sorrows of war."

In the spring of 1944, Roddie and the 106th Infantry Division moved from Fort Jackson, South Carolina, to Camp

Atterbury, Indiana, an arduous six-hundred-mile trip as they prepared to ship out to Europe. Roddie continued to train new troops because the ranks of the 106th Division had been depleted by a steady need for replacement troops in other divisions. In the course of the war, no other infantry division would lose as many men before entering combat as the Golden Lions. Between September 1943 and its entry into combat, the 106th had 12,442 men reassigned to other divisions, 80 percent of its total.

The Allied high command coordinated the military efforts of the Allied forces, including the United States. In 1944, the leadership began the top secret planning for the D-Day invasion, a massive effort to storm the beaches of Normandy, France, where the Germans were. The US Army decided that it needed millions of frontline fighters rather than college-trained specialists and officers, like those in the ASTP. In February 1944, the army ended the ASTP, and the soldiers in that program went into the infantry, airborne, and armored divisions.

These former ASTP soldiers didn't get special treatment. Despite their intellect and credentials, few gained the chance to attend Officer Candidate School. They often received a harsh welcome from the regular infantrymen, who considered them just a bunch of college kids who needed to be taught about the rough reality in the "real" army.

But Roddie saw things differently. When he met Private

Skip Friedman and others who were from the ASTP, he realized they had smarts and knew a lot of things like communications and engineering, which could help in a combat situation. He considered his division lucky to have these capable young soldiers. Skip appreciated Roddie's respect. "Some of the noncoms—noncommissioned officers—were shouters, but Roddie was different," Skip said. "He was a terrific guy. Quiet, and reserved, just a very steady guy. You could count on him, he was totally dependable. He led by example."

Throughout 1944, Roddie helped rebuild the 106th Division with replacements from different army units. Replacements were needed after the Allied invasion of Europe on D-Day. "We lost so many men during the D-Day invasion—and the demand for replacements from the infantry was so high—that the army decided to take all men who had not completed training in the air corps and reassign them to combat units," Lester recalled. That's how he was reunited with the 106th Division, which was in the final stage of preparing to go overseas. Lester was no longer an air cadet, but he was promoted to sergeant in the infantry.

Roddie tried to prepare his men for battle. He knew that no matter how well he trained them, they would likely have no idea what to expect during the brutality of land warfare in Europe.

At the same time that he was preparing his troops, Roddie

was coping with a personal crisis. Earlier that summer, he had received divorce papers from his wife, Marie. "When my wife divorced me, I almost went crazy," he wrote. "Everyone told me it was best, but I didn't care what everyone thought. I only knew it wasn't right with God."

On July 30, Roddie was granted ten days' leave from his army duties to travel back to Knoxville to attempt to save his marriage before he left for battle. It didn't work; the divorce was finalized on August 5. He returned to Fort Jackson five days early. "I had lost what I had wanted all my life, a home, a wife, and happiness," he wrote. "I was a pretty weary guy when I got back to camp. Frankie seemed to know what was going on in my mind and he tried his best to make me forget."

While he didn't forget, he went back to work, leading his men as they all prepared for war.

8
THE TWENTY-EIGHTH DIVISION

I arrived in Washington, DC, on October 29, 2013, on a fact-finding mission. I was becoming a history detective, spending hours at the National Archives in College Park, Maryland, and at the Library of Congress in Washington, DC, researching the 106th Division and its heroic role in the Battle of the Bulge.

I found page upon page that I couldn't look away from— it was like some real-life thriller—jigsaw-puzzle pieces from German stalag records and postwar testimony from newly liberated POWs. As a POW at Ziegenhain, my dad wrote at one point, "I'm just a little guy," but I could see now that he'd been swept up in an epic and defining moment in the twentieth century.

What I was most excited about was that I'd lined up a meeting with a former POW named Paul Stern, who lived with his wife, Corinne, in Reston, Virginia, about a thirty-minute drive east of the nation's capital. I knew Paul was another vital link, an eyewitness who'd known my father well.

When I arrived, I found an eighty-nine-year-old man who was alert, animated, and clearheaded. He was dressed in a black sweater and a white oxford shirt and wore tinted wire-rimmed glasses. As I scrambled to get my video recorder going, Paul rushed to tell me of his experiences in the war, his arrival in France, only weeks after the D-Day invasion.

While Roddie was still in the United States training the troops, Paul Stern was in France serving as an army medic. "Our job was to help the wounded on the battlefield, to save those soldiers," Paul said. "Shells dropping all over. People getting killed all around you. It was just a different life, but you had to adjust to that life. And not to say that we got *used* to it—it was scary—but you had to adjust to it. Within twenty-four hours, you were changed. You were a different person."

Paul was born on January 27, 1924. Like Lester, Paul and his family lived in a Jewish section of the South Bronx. His father and mother, Max and Jennie, had emigrated from Austria. Max had steady work as a tailor, even during the worst days of the Great Depression. Paul loved playing stickball in the street in front of his house. He was extremely bright, outgoing, and optimistic. He listened to opera on the radio and sang tenor with the German glee club.

He graduated from high school near the top of his class and earned a scholarship to Wesleyan University. He turned it down to attend City College in New York, but then he enlisted in the army. He began training as a dental technician, but his superiors recognized his abilities and transferred him into a program for combat medics. "Guys with the highest IQs they put in [to be] the medics," Paul said. "On the battlefield, in an emergency, you had to be able to think fast."

Paul arrived in France in July 1944 and was assigned to the Twenty-Eighth Infantry Division, the oldest division-sized unit in the US Armed Forces. As a combat medic, he was immediately thrust into the chaos of battle. He tried to pick up some tricks of survival from infantrymen with a few weeks' more experience in combat. Paul learned how to respond to a Nazi artillery attack. "We would jump into a shell hole because we knew another shell wouldn't come to the same hole," he said. "You were safe in that hole. We learned that almost right away. It was a strange thing: jumping into a fresh shell hole to be safe."

US Army medics were under constant enemy fire, but they didn't carry any arms themselves. Medics were distinguished by wearing red armbands, which made Paul feel he was marked for death. "If the Germans wanted to shoot us, they could just aim for the red armbands," Paul said.

In his early days in France, Paul became good friends with another combat medic from Chicago. He recalled the day he watched his friend die: "We had a wounded soldier on a litter. I picked up the back end and my buddy was in the front. As we rose, a sniper shot my friend through the head. Like that, just snuffed him out." Paul later wrote to his friend's parents, telling them what a noble and able man their son had been.

By the summer of 1944, the Nazi concentration camps were being exposed to the world. On July 23, Soviet soldiers captured Majdanek, the first of the Nazi death camps, located in eastern Poland. Seeing the camp's high walls, large metal gate, brick buildings, smokestacks, and barracks, the Soviets had assumed it was some kind of factory. They didn't imagine it was a factory of death. When the Soviet soldiers opened the doors to a gas chamber, they found the crematorium had just been used.

It took many months for a disbelieving world to come to grips with the horrific news. The *New York Times* sent its veteran war correspondent, W. H. "Bill" Lawrence, to Poland so he could see the evidence for himself. Lawrence's stunning report ran on the front page of the newspaper on August 30, 1944, under a banner headline:

NAZI MASS KILLING LAID BARE IN CAMP
Victims Put at 1,500,000 in Huge Death Factory of Gas Chambers and Crematories

For millions of Americans, it was the first news account of a crime so vast, grotesque, and industrialized that it still had no name. For the first time, the world heard journalists describe canisters of deadly gas, more than eight hundred thousand pairs of shoes found in a camp warehouse, and gas chambers disguised as showers. They found passports and identification papers showing that many of the murdered were small children and the elderly, and that Jews had been "brought to the camp to be exterminated from literally every country in Europe, from Poland to Holland."

Bill Lawrence's lead in the *Times* was stark and unequivocal:

"I have just seen the most terrible place on the face of the earth—the German concentration camp at Majdanek . . . in which it is estimated by Soviet and Polish authorities that as many as 1,500,000 persons from nearly every country in Europe were killed in the last three years." (Holocaust scholars now estimate that several hundred thousand people died at the camp.)

From Normandy, Paul and the others in the Twenty-Eighth Division started for Paris in an operation known as Operation Cobra. This was for British, Canadian, and American forces to secure areas of France. As part of Operation Cobra, Paul and his division marched from Normandy toward Paris, passing roads littered with abandoned tanks and the corpses of men and horses.

As they completed Operation Cobra, on August 29, 1944, Paul and the other men in the Twenty-Eighth Division participated in the liberation of Paris, a march down the Champs-Élysées to the Arc de Triomphe in Paris. "We were chosen to be the division to parade through Paris," Paul said. "They later put it on a postage stamp. As we paraded under the Arc de Triomphe, you could see that [General] Eisenhower was there with [French president Charles] de Gaulle and all the generals. It was quite a scene."

But they didn't have time to rest or celebrate. The Twenty-Eighth Division went from the parade into battle, driving the Germans toward the Belgian border. "We chased the Germans the next day," Paul said. "And we kept chasing them. At various times we'd engage the enemy and we'd have a quick fight."

Finally, in early September, during a period of rest, Paul asked his commander if he could go see his brother, Jack, in southern France. To his surprise, he was able to find his brother. "Imagine! I found one soldier in the *entire* division. No one would believe it. I was so driven. I found Jack. I have pictures of the two of us. We were both together in uniform." After a few days, Paul returned to his post with the Twenty-Eighth Division.

At that point, Paul and his brother, Jack, as well as many of the other soldiers, had started to relax. After a long string of Allied victories, it seemed like the war was winding down. They thought the war was almost won.

9
VICTORY FEVER

By the fall of 1944, the Allied powers were becoming confident. As Paul Stern and other soldiers with the Twenty-Eighth Division saw firsthand, the Nazis were retreating rapidly in France, and they were losing to the Soviets on the Eastern Front. After the liberation of Paris, General Dwight Eisenhower—the commander of the Allied forces—moved his headquarters to the Palace of Versailles, just outside Paris.

"Militarily, the war is over," Eisenhower's chief of staff, Lieutenant General Walter Bedell Smith, told the press in late summer. In September, British prime minister Winston Churchill said, "Victory is *everywhere*. I would not be surprised . . . if the enemy surrenders in weeks." The following day, Allied forces crossed the Siegfried Line—a German defense line—and occupied German soil.

But the celebrations were premature. General George

Patton and Britain's Field Marshal Bernard Law Montgomery were racing to be the first commander to take Berlin, and in their hurry they both got ahead of their supply lines, making it difficult to get tanks refueled and to restock other supplies they needed. The Germans held their ground in defense of the deepwater port in Antwerp, Belgium, leading to a fierce and deadly battle.

Still, Germany seemed on the verge of surrender. Field Marshal Montgomery bet Eisenhower that his 21st Army Group would be marching through the streets of Berlin by Christmas.

Many young American soldiers still in training thought that the fighting might be over before they were even deployed. One of those men was Irwin "Sonny" Fox. He remembered that when he heard about the D-Day invasion, he thought the war would be over before he could catch up to it.

Sonny was a six-foot-three, rail-thin, first-generation Jewish kid from Flatbush, Brooklyn. He loved stickball and watching the Dodgers play baseball at Ebbets Field. He was a freshman at New York University studying theater and hosting his own college radio show when he was called up to the US Army. "I got the draft notice shortly after I turned eighteen and I reported in for the draft exam," Sonny said. "And they found me totally acceptable: I was breathing."

In fact, Sonny scored high on the aptitude test and was

chosen for fast-track basic training at Fort Benning, Georgia. He had never been outside New York, so Sonny was shocked by the treatment of black soldiers, noting that black and white soldiers could not even ride the same buses or serve in the same platoons. More than one million African Americans served in segregated divisions and combat support roles such as cook or quartermaster during World War II. "The Great War to save democracy," he said, "was being fought by a totally segregated US Army."

Sonny was sent to England aboard the commandeered *Queen Elizabeth* luxury liner. The grand ship was "double loaded" with twenty thousand soldiers. Eighteen men were squeezed into cabins built for two. After the crowded journey, Sonny crossed England and went to Belgium. On October 23, 1944, he wrote to his parents in Brooklyn.

Dearest Folks,

I'm sitting right now on Belgian soil (and my own posterior) under a shelter of pine limbs, next to a warm fire, in the coals of which are roasting some potatoes. I've just finished a good hot meal, augmented substantially by one of the occasional cow or deer which "accidentally" strayed in the line of fire of one of the men. Of course, if someone should say I could go home, there would be a puff of dust and a flash of speed and Brooklyn here I'd come!

Sonny "caught up with the war" along the German-Belgian border, where he replaced another soldier in the Twenty-Eighth Division. "The policy of the military was to feed in replacements as the war wore on," Sonny said. "When we were lined up to enter the ranks of Company E, 110th Regiment, Twenty-Eighth Infantry Division, not one of the men in this particular gaggle had ever met the other." Because Sonny had spent eleven months in the army, he was considered "experienced." As such, he was given the position of squad leader, in charge of eleven men. He was nineteen years old.

Before pushing into Germany, the Twenty-Eighth Division and other US forces were ordered to get rid of any resistance from the area of the Hürtgen Forest. Nothing could have prepared Sonny, Paul Stern, or any of the other men of the Twenty-Eighth Division for the horror they were about to encounter. Even the seasoned older German officers called the fighting in the Hürtgen "worse than anything in the First World War."

"The Hürtgen Forest sat along the German-Belgian border, about fifty square miles of dense woods, with tall fir trees that blocked the sun," Sonny said. "It was a dark and eerie place where the thick lower branches of the fir trees were only two feet off the ground. The forest floor never got any sunlight."

On November 2, 1944, the Twenty-Eighth Division entered the forest. The German defenders were ready and well-positioned. They immediately pinned down the US troops using mortar and artillery fire. After two days of fighting, the Allied forces had only moved one mile. Harsh early winter weather grounded any air support, which might have been able to help.

Sonny arrived at the front in the middle of the night and heard the other soldiers complaining about the German 88-mm artillery, which was as accurate as rifle fire but could also be fired from a great distance. "As we were walking up to the first positions under fire, I felt a combination of fear and elation," he wrote later. "Fear of what might happen—elation that I was okay. That first walk up there was the first time I'd ever been under fire. I found out that I could make it. When my squad moved into its position in the Hürtgen, we weren't even told where the enemy was. Being responsible for eleven other guys was very important to me. It was raining and cold, a damp, penetrating cold that went through your bones. Nighttime was frequently below freezing, and damp and fog was everywhere. I had one change of socks, which never dried, so my feet wouldn't stay warm."

As they stood their ground, the Nazi artillerymen had perfected a tactic to maximize injury. "The Germans had timed the fuses on their shells to explode at treetop level, thus dispersing the deadly shrapnel over a wide area," Sonny said. "A substantial number of our casualties were from this shellfire."

"In the Hürtgen Forest," Paul Stern remembered, "the way the shells would go off, hitting the treetop, spreading the shell, it could kill you when you were a half a mile away. The shell and fractured tree parts would spread out. It was *hell*. We thought we were all dead men. Every day we woke up in the forest we didn't know if we would make it to the next day."

The battle of the Hürtgen ended in a major victory for the Germans.

More than thirty-three thousand American troops were killed or wounded during the battle, representing an astonishing 25 percent casualty rate. Sonny and Paul's Twenty-Eighth Division suffered 6,184 combat casualties, plus 728 cases of trench foot and 620 cases of "battle fatigue," or post-traumatic stress disorder in today's terminology.

Many of the soldiers who survived Hürtgen never spoke of the battle again.

While the Twenty-Eighth Division was mired in the Hürtgen Forest, Roddie and the men of the 106th were completing their final training at Camp Atterbury in Indiana. Roddie had led his men through intensive combat drills and taught them to use and care for their M1 rifles.

Roddie and the other soldiers undoubtedly heard reports of the Nazi crimes against Soviet prisoners of war and civilians in eastern Poland, which must have strengthened their resolve. This was no longer simply warfare; it was a fight to save the world from murderous tyranny. Jewish soldiers—young men such as Lester and Skip—must have realized that wearing army-issued dog tags stamped with *H* for Hebrew identifying their religion put them at risk if they were captured by the Nazis.

Roddie and his men continued to train, then left for Scotland in October 1944. From Scotland, they headed south by trains and trucks into the English Midlands, where they joined with the rest of the division outside the small city of Cheltenham. The officers of the 106th Infantry Division were told that their men were being given an "easy" posting in an area so uneventful that the soldiers had nicknamed it the "Ghost Front."

According to the official Army Morning Report of November 30, 1944: "Departed by rail 0130 for Southampton. Weather cold and clear. Morale good."

10
GHOST FRONT

The war had been going on for five years now, and the situation was looking bleak for the Germans. The Allies hoped that the war would wind down by the end of 1944. However, the Nazis continued to put up a fight. Operation Market Garden was an American mission launched in September 1944 that ended in a tragic loss of life. The plan was designed to capture nine crucial bridges that would have provided a clear Allied route into Germany. The Allies succeeded in liberating the Dutch cities of Eindhoven and Nijmegen, but they were unable to capture the last bridge over the Rhine River. During the nine-day operation, at least seventeen thousand Allied troops were killed, wounded, or missing in action.

The failure of Operation Market Garden coupled with the horrific loss of life in the Hürtgen Forest brought a grim change of mood to the troops. The war wasn't over, not by a long shot. In addition, the Allies were having trouble keeping frontline troops supplied with food, fuel, arms, ammunition, and winter clothing. They couldn't bring in enough provisions at the Normandy beaches to meet operational needs. They had control of only one deepwater port, and the Germans had mined the harbor and destroyed the docks before retreating. In the first days of September, the Allies captured a second port—the port at Antwerp—but it would not be fully operational until late November.

It didn't seem possible to reach Berlin and end the war in Europe by Christmas. Instead, the war on the Western Front had become a steady battle against an increasingly desperate and battle-hardened enemy. Adolf Hitler tried to restore optimism among the German forces, so he told his men he had a bold plan. He ordered German troops to drive through the dense forest of the Ardennes, then go north to recapture the port at Antwerp. He thought he could surround and destroy a number of Allied forces, possibly creating enough political tension to destroy the Western alliance.

Hitler's generals didn't think the plan could work, but they didn't say anything. "It was obvious to me that the available forces were far too small—no soldier really believed that the aim of reaching Antwerp was really practicable," said one German officer. "But I knew that it was useless to protest to Hitler about . . . anything."

The officers of the high command tried to explain the enormous manpower advantage held by the US Army. But

Hitler didn't think the US Army could *fight*. Hitler viewed America as a weak "mongrel" nation made up of all sorts of different races. Hitler didn't understand that the *diversity* of the United States, and divisions like the Golden Lions, was its greatest strength.

In December, the Allies reached the German border and stopped. Thousands of Allied forces were positioned along the Siegfried Line—about 690 kilometers (430 miles) of concrete guard posts, barbed wire, tank traps, and foxholes. All along that front, also known as the "Westwall," things were unchanging—and winter weather was on its way.

The Germans dug in and waited for the Allies to attack. On the Eastern Front, they braced for an attack from the Soviets, which they expected as soon as the muddy earth froze solid enough to support the Soviet tanks.

The Allies heard occasional machine-gun bursts and heavy-weapon fire, and periodically they would see a German combat patrol. That was the extent of the military action, even though parts of the US Army were, in fact, occupying German soil. It seemed like the kind of stalemate common in World War I.

On December 2, 1944, Roddie, Lester, Frankie, and the other men of the 106th Division made landfall in France on the Normandy coast. Each man climbed down rope netting onto landing barges, which pitched and heaved in the cold North Atlantic surf. The men carried full field packs, helmet, rifle, loaded cartridge belt, and two additional bandoleers of ammunition. When the barge got close to the shore, the men jumped into the surf and staggered ashore.

The night of his arrival, Lester wrote a letter to his older brother Paul, who was serving with the US Army Transportation Corps in New York City. Lester wanted Paul and his family to know he had arrived safely in France and that all was well. His words were optimistic and encouraging, just as he had intended. Though he would be heading to the front soon, he assured them he would be stationed in a "quiet sector." No cause for alarm. And besides, Lester wrote, the French seemed like "fine people and fun to know." Like many others, Lester thought the war was wrapping up, and he expected to be home by the end of the year. He wrote that he looked forward to enjoying his mother's onion rolls and cream cheese after taking care of some business with Hitler.

Shivering and soaked, the men of the 106th began a long trek toward the front. They traveled in uncovered trucks, through freezing rain and snow, across France and Belgium. By December 9, all regiments of the division were scheduled to reach the Ardennes Forest, near the ancient town of Saint Vith in Belgium. It was a harsh welcome to life in the field.

Roddie's 422nd Regiment arrived in the pitch-dark. The

heavy snowfall and the restricted use of lights made it very difficult for the men to follow their guides. Some soldiers were separated from their units and became lost in the dense woods.

Roddie and his men found themselves at the center of the Allied front, in the heart of the Ardennes, the sprawling hilly woodlands that rolled through parts of France, Belgium, Germany, and Luxembourg. The Ardennes was old-growth pine forest, dense and dark. There were only a few small towns nearby; most of the landscape consisted of trackless woods, rolling hills, steep ravines, and ridges. The locals in their area were mostly of German descent, but there were also some Belgians. Many towns had divided loyalties, with some supporting the Nazis and others active in the resistance.

The 106th Division took up positions on a long thin front just outside Saint Vith, at the Schnee Eifel, or "Snow Mountain." The area was characterized by high plateaus, deep valleys, and limited roads. Due to the snow and ice, some of the roads were almost impassable at the time. Although most armies labeled the Ardennes "impenetrable," militaries had, in fact, traveled through it for years, from the early Romans to Hitler's army in 1940. They could get through, but it wouldn't be easy.

When Roddie and the men of the 106th arrived at Snow

Mountain, the weather was cold, and the ground covered with ice and fresh snow. The sky was cloudy, and snow flurries limited visibility; a thick mist hung over the treetops. The scene looked like a Christmas card. It reminded Roddie of the hills and hollers of East Tennessee.

Everything was quiet, almost too quiet. The inexperienced 106th Division had been assigned to the Ardennes so that the troops could ease into fighting. No one expected them to see much action. The 106th was the last American infantry division to be mobilized during World War II. It was also the youngest; two-thirds of its troops were single men under the age of twenty-three.

The 106th had been ordered to swap places with the exhausted Second Infantry Division, man for man, across a twenty-eight-mile sector. When the soldiers of the 106th piled out of their muddy trucks, they were met by dozens of bearded, ragged, stinking, dirty infantrymen who hadn't showered in weeks. To the rookie troops of the 106th, the men of the Second Division looked almost savage, grinning knowingly at the new kids. Some of the veteran infantrymen offered sarcastic and profane best wishes as they piled into trucks to be taken away from the front lines.

"It's been so quiet up here," one regimental commander of the Second had told the regimental commander of the

106th, "your men will learn the easy way." Roddie was told by his commanding officer that the first few weeks on Snow Mountain would "be a piece of cake."

At dawn on the morning of December 10, Roddie and his men prepared to move to the front lines. When they arrived, the men of the 106th took up positions in foxholes, mostly prepared by the Second Division and largely filled with mud and water. The terrain was treacherous: minefields and barbed-wire entanglements were in front of them. Additional mines and trip flares were hidden in the gaps between occupied positions.

Skip Friedman recalled that they were right on top of the Nazi fortifications, actually on the German side of the border. "Within a few days, we replaced the Second Division, company by company on the front," Skip said. "We were among the first troops on the German side of the border."

But the soldiers had to worry about more than enemy gunfire and land mines. The winter of 1944 to 1945 would prove to be one of the coldest and wettest ever recorded in Europe. The damp and unsanitary conditions left the men vulnerable to trench foot, a painful disease in which poor blood circulation destroys the tissues in the feet and toes, often requiring amputation. Before the men had reached Snow Mountain, dozens of men from the 106th had to be evacuated because they suffered from trench foot. "Both the enemy and weather could kill you," one private said. "And the two of them together was a pretty deadly combination."

As promised, the first few days in at Snow Mountain were routine for Roddie and the rest of the division. Then the men began to hear rumbling sounds, much like the noises of tanks, trucks, and other armored vehicles. When they asked their superiors about the sounds, their warnings were dismissed as an overreaction of new arrivals.

The noises increased. Soldiers reported the whistle of steam locomotives and reconnaissance planes flying over their positions. As the communications chief for Headquarters Company, Roddie notified his commanding officers about the heavy-equipment noises and suspected troop movements, but his warnings were downplayed.

When the 106th's commander, Major General Jones, told his superiors at VIII Corps headquarters he himself was hearing armor, he got a blunt reply: "Don't be so jumpy, General."

All reports sent up the intelligence chain by the 106th were chalked up to "nerves." Men of the 106th were even told that the Germans might be "playing recorded sounds" of tanks over loudspeakers to spook the new men. The failure to take the warnings seriously was one of the most massive military intelligence failures of the entire war.

The sounds were real. Hitler was carrying out the bold plan he had imagined. Under the cover of heavy fog, hidden in the thick pine forest, the Germans had amassed seven tank and thirteen infantry divisions for the opening attack.

Two days before the fighting began, Lester's brother, Paul Tannenbaum, responded to Lester's letter.

Thursday—14 December 1944

Dear Les,

Received your letter written from France on the 4th of December. Your letters are cheerful and full of good spirits and one can't feel badly long when you get so much of your energy into the written word. The mention of "onion rolls and cream cheese" has stirred Mother to action. In most of the future packages that she will send out you will probably find close facsimile of either or both. She is kind of worried, though, over the fact that you haven't received any of the other packages. I guess they will catch up with you in time—although Mother is inclined to believe they fell into the hands of the enemy and because of these extra provisions the war is being prolonged.

Of course, the news that you are in France . . . is not conducive to happy feelings. But sitting down and thinking it all out logically—a hard task—there's not much one can do—except fight all the harder to make this damn war

business over and done with. There's a great deal of living for
you to catch up with and it irks me something awful to see you
wasting years . . .
Keep well, Les.

Always,
Paul

Lester never received his brother's letter in the Ardennes.

11
ATTACK

The massive winter attack against the Allies was named Operation Watch on the Rhine. Hitler had initially planned for the mission to begin in late November, when cold fog usually blankets the Ardennes Forest, but the plan was delayed due to Nazi fuel shortages. By mid-December—just after the 106th Division arrived—they were ready to carry out their plan.

Hitler wanted to direct the massive operation from his western headquarters in central Germany. Unknown to Allied military intelligence or even the local townspeople, Hitler had built a secret compound known as Adlerhorst, "Eagle's Nest." The compound looked like an innocent group of seven wooden country cottages with second-story dormers. Many even had wooden porches decorated with flower baskets. But they were actually bunkers with three-foot-thick walls and ceilings of reinforced concrete.

Planning for the mission had been conducted with great secrecy. All the generals had been forced to sign an oath that they would receive the death penalty if they leaked any information. Late on the afternoon of December 11, buses brought divisional commanders to the Eagle's Nest to be personally briefed by Hitler about the offensive. Before entering, each officer had to be searched and had to surrender both his gun and his briefcase.

The führer's paranoia was full-blown following a failed assassination attempt the previous July. Some within his party wanted to take control of the armed forces and negotiate a peace treaty. Hitler no longer trusted many of his generals. He put his faith in the SS troops—the Schutzstaffel—a military-like group that defended Hitler and the Nazi Party. Many generals thought Hitler's behavior was unpredictable; those who had not seen him since the assassination attempt were shocked to see that Hitler was pale, stooped over, and that his left arm trembled uncontrollably.

Finally, Hitler announced the details of the attack: at 5:30 a.m. on December 16, German forces would attack the Allies at Snow Mountain. The Allies were vastly outnumbered. Hitler had gathered 410,000 troops, 1,400 tanks, and 2,600 artillery weapons for the predawn offensive. Using the element of surprise and the bad weather—which would prevent the Allies from using their powerful air defenses—his divisions would push through the forest, cross the bridges at the river Meuse, and recapture the port of Antwerp. This attack would also split the Allied forces in northern France. The Allies would be caught completely off guard.

"This battle is to decide whether we shall live or die," Hitler said. "I want all my soldiers to fight hard and without pity. The battle must be fought with brutality and all resistance must be broken in a wave of terror. In this most serious hour of the Fatherland, I expect every one of my soldiers to be courageous and again courageous. The enemy must be beaten—now! Thus lives our Germany!" Hitler added: "The enemy can never reckon upon us surrendering. Never! Never!"

The attack would be led by Joseph "Sepp" Dietrich, one of Hitler's closest supporters. Dietrich had been a sergeant in World War I and later founded an SS unit that served as Hitler's personal army. He now led the Sixth Panzer (tank) Army. Many generals didn't respect Dietrich because of his rough manner and stormtrooper background; he acted more like a bully than a military leader. Still, he was chosen by Hitler to lead the attack.

The commander of the Fifth Panzer Army, General Hasso von Manteuffel, did have the respect of his fellow military leaders. Manteuffel was small—about five feet tall, with a slight build—but he was a decorated combat officer in World War I. He was known as tough-minded and unafraid to confront Hitler. Manteuffel was ordered to have his men circle Snow Mountain, trapping the American 106th Division. Other troops would take the surrounding towns, as well as those to the south, to block any attempt by the Allies to send in reinforcements.

This mission would be unlike any other seen on the Western Front. Hitler gave a great deal of responsibility to his trusted SS, many of whom were by now veterans of the savage killing fields of the Eastern Front. One commander who characterized the inhumanity of Nazi warfare was twenty-nine-year-old Joachim Peiper. Even by the standards of the SS, Peiper was considered ruthless. He had enlisted in the SS at age nineteen and trained at Dachau, Germany's first concentration camp. He led several invasions in which he encircled and burned entire villages, killing all the inhabitants, earning his SS unit the nickname the "Blowtorch Battalion." He and his men gunned down soldiers rather than taking them as prisoners of war. As a young commander of his own group, Peiper and his troops committed some of the most heartless and infamous acts of World War II.

Hitler wanted to make sure that his bold winter mission included his favorite SS commander, Otto Skorzeny. Skorzeny stood six feet, four inches tall. He was powerfully built, with deep scars on his left cheek from a fencing duel. By December 1944, Skorzeny had already achieved a mythical status within the ranks of the German military for his against-all-odds rescue of Benito Mussolini during a daring air raid.

"Skorzeny," Hitler said, "this next assignment will be the most important of your life." Hitler considered Skorzeny the only man he could trust with the success of this top secret command mission. Operation Griffin, the brainchild of Adolf Hitler, aimed to capture the strategically vital bridges over the Meuse River in Belgium and to confuse the enemy.

"I want you to command a group of American troops and get them across the Meuse and seize one of the bridges. Not, my dear Skorzeny, real Americans. I want you to create special units wearing American uniforms. They will travel in captured Allied tanks. Think of the confusion you could cause! I envisage a whole string of false orders which will upset communications and attack morale."

Hitler granted Skorzeny virtually unlimited authority to prepare his mission. Using tactics entirely illegal under international laws of warfare, his soldiers would dress in authentic US Army uniforms, drive captured jeeps and Sherman tanks, and sabotage equipment on the Allied side.

First, they looked for German officers who spoke English with American accents. Those who passed the language test were told they would be part of a special unit called the 150th Panzer Brigade. They were commanded to sign a secrecy order, any violation of which would be punishable by death.

The Germans had collected more than two thousand American uniforms from prisoner-of-war camps. Skorzeny selected one hundred and fifty men. They wore American uniforms and learned to salute in the American style. For months, every order was given in English. Training included watching Hollywood movies to learn up-to-date slang, and even "how to tap their cigarette against the pack in an American way." Anyone who questioned the mission was threatened with execution.

Once they crossed the American lines, the fake Americans of the 150th Panzer Brigade would make trouble: they would destroy bridges, cut telephone wires, start fires at ammunition dumps and fuel stores, send false orders to US units, reverse road signs, remove minefield warnings, and block roads with warnings of nonexistent mines. They would make chaos.

By December 14, the Germans were ready. Word of the German offensive had leaked out, but the Allies didn't take it seriously. The idea of a massive wintertime offensive in the west seemed too far-fetched to be true.

The Allies underestimated Hitler's control of the German Armed Forces, and the Allied commanders also miscalculated their opponents. Senior American officers believed that because they wouldn't attack under such unfavorable conditions, the Nazis wouldn't either. This failure of intelligence gathering, strategic understanding, and basic psychology of Hitler would prove tragic.

12
TERROR

At 5:30 a.m. on December 16, the earth erupted. In an instant, pine trees exploded into lethal wooden spikes, and the frigid air turned fiery red.

Roddie jolted from sleep, clung to the shaking, icy ground, and desperately crawled toward his helmet as German artillery rained down with pinpoint accuracy from every direction. Terrain and weather were no longer his greatest enemies. His enemies were the blasts and deadly shrapnel.

There was nowhere to run or hide. Across the valley were thousands of enemy troops, with thundering tanks and heavy artillery.

Fear was also Roddie's enemy. Fear that he would be blown to pieces in an instant. Fear for the lives of his boys and what they were experiencing. Fear that he might not make it home, might never see his family again.

This was a terror Roddie never could have imagined. He knew panic was lethal to an infantryman, but it gripped him with a sickening embrace. His body shivered as he shook off thoughts of his own death.

The treetop-explosion technique perfected in the Hürtgen Forest was being put to devastating effect now in the Ardennes. Every tree in the forest seemed to have been blasted from its roots at the same time. Months of training could not have prepared Roddie and his men for the horrific reality of battle. He fought the urge to run. All around him, wounded men screamed. Fiery shrapnel dropped around him as he crawled toward a pile of the sandbags enclosing the communications station. Roddie reached for his radio. Dazed, he called Regimental Command to let them know the intensity of the attack and the frightening accuracy of the Nazi 88s.

Drawing heavy fire, all sectors. Lines down. I and R. Five MIA. Request support.

He repeated the message several times, but heard no response.

Finally, Roddie's radio crackled to life. *Don't be jumpy. Ghost front position. Likely "social calls." Hold position.*

Roddie's commanding officers downplayed the incoming reports as an overreaction from a green (inexperienced) division.

During a brief moment of quiet, Roddie stepped outside

for a breath of fresh air only to hear a whistle—the sound of a bullet whizzing past inches above his head. In his journal he described the near-fatal moment:

> *Boy, I was thankful the Lord was on my side. And I didn't hesitate to tell him either. I prayed hot and heavy and was convinced of that old saying—that there are no atheists in a foxhole.*

In the chaos, it felt like the end of the world.

"Our little village of Schlausenbach was hit time and time again," Lester said. "The houses no longer looked secure, and we were digging ourselves into the foundations and into the ground." In that moment, every soldier picked up a gun and became a rifleman. "I can still see Butch, our Headquarters Company cook, dashing around in the jeep and firing his machine gun like mad," Lester wrote. "None of us knew how serious the situation had become."

The dreaded 88-mm artillery shells "bored through the darkness at half a mile per second, as if hugging the Ardennes hills." Rockets the soldiers called "Screaming Meemies" zipped through the woods, breaking up the steady sound of machine-gun fire.

Roddie then heard the low groan of tanks and the clanking roars of armored vehicles as Hitler's army burst forward through the forest. His radio was out. He found that the

Nazis had jammed the radio frequencies and severed the telephone wires, making communication impossible.

The attack continued for close to an hour. Then the German soldiers began to advance across the open fields in what appeared to be a column of platoons in line. Allied riflemen and machine gunners opened fire. By about 10:00 a.m., the fighting briefly stopped.

Small patrols of Germans made their way through the company lines. One group, camouflaged in white snowsuits, reached one hundred yards from the command post before they were stopped.

German prisoners were sent to Battalion Headquarters for questioning. One captured German officer carried a written copy of the attack order. The Allies were stunned to learn that the attack was part of a massive German counteroffensive.

The Allied troops were outnumbered. The attack has been described as being "like wolves on a sheepfold, falling on an American regiment at an unnerving ratio of ten wolves for each sheep." The American forces were stretched thin, so the German forces didn't have much trouble breaking the line and surrounding the men of the 106th.

Roddie and the 422nd put up heroic resistance. On the battlefield, they were transformed from teenagers into men, battling the German attack with brains as well as brawn.

Roddie was proud of all of his boys; they were brave in the face of death.

But the Twenty-Eighth Infantry Division was also overwhelmed. They were tasked with holding a twenty-five-mile front along the Our River. Instead of facing two German divisions across the river, as army intelligence had reported, the men of the Twenty-Eighth found themselves fighting five full divisions, plus heavy enemy reinforcements.

The German artillerymen had excellent intelligence on the US troops. They knew that the soldiers preferred to sleep in the homes of villagers, rather than in foxholes, so many of the initial artillery bursts fell on civilian houses.

Sonny Fox found that out firsthand. He was bunking in a farmhouse when he was awakened by the sound of artillery screeching overhead. He ran to the foxhole a few yards away.

"How long has this been going on?" he asked.

"About twenty minutes."

Sonny started back to the house to get the rest of his squad out.

"As I got close to the door," he said, "I heard an incoming and dove under the butcher block alongside the entrance. The shell passed over. I tried to get out, but I couldn't move. The battle was beginning, and I was stuck under a butcher block! I finally broke loose and dashed into the house to find my mighty band of warriors cowering in the potato cellar. I shouted them out of there and into our prepared positions on both sides of the farmhouse."

After about ten minutes, the artillery barrage stopped. Strange green signal lights arched into the sky against the thick cloud cover.

Sonny heard Germans walking down the road on the other side of the hedge that separated him from that road. As they approached, Sonny pulled the pin from a grenade. He looked up and saw three soldiers strolling along. He tossed the grenade in their direction and ducked into the foxhole to avoid the explosion. Less than five seconds later, the grenade went off.

Later that afternoon, Sonny heard tanks coming down the road. He didn't know if they were German or American. "They turned out to be ours, and I thought we had beaten them off, but the captain said no, the Germans were behind us and the fighting was going on well behind our lines."

Huge numbers of German troops and tanks were well to the rear of the Allied lines. Some were also masquerading as US soldiers and making a mess of Allied communications. By switching around road signs, they sent an entire US regiment in the wrong direction.

Once the Americans learned that Germans were behind the line, the army set up checkpoints. The soldiers began questioning everyone—even high-ranking officers—on facts they felt only real Americans would know, such as details about baseball, US geography, and popular comic book villains.

For the most part, the roadblocks failed, even though they captured a few German commandos.

American soldiers shot out the tires on a British field marshal's jeep after he refused to stop at a bridge checkpoint. Brigadier General Bruce Clarke was held at gunpoint for five hours after he incorrectly told military policemen the Chicago Cubs played in the American League.

"But I'm General Bruce Clarke!" he shouted.

"Like hell!" the soldier yelled. "You're one of Skorzeny's men. We were told to watch out for a [German] posing as a one-star general."

Even Clarke's commander, General Omar Bradley, was repeatedly stopped at checkpoints. "Three times I was ordered to prove my identity," Bradley said.

Many of the fake Americans were finally caught in the effort, but in the confusion the US Army began to see spies and German assassins everywhere. "A half million [soldiers] played cat and mouse with each other each time they met on the road," Bradley said. "Neither rank nor credentials spared the traveler an inquisition at each intersection he passed." Two US soldiers were even reported to have been shot by a trigger-happy US military policeman who was convinced they were Germans in disguise.

* * *

The Americans were confused. Unsure of how to proceed, Major General Jones, commander of the 106th, asked advice from Major General Troy Middleton, commander of VIII Corps. Jones wasn't getting updated reports from the front lines because of the communications problems. He didn't know that the Fourteenth Cavalry Group, which had been protecting the 106th, had retreated after suffering major losses. Jones asked Middleton if he should order the 106th to pull back.

"You know how things are up there better than I do," Middleton said in a crackling phone call from his headquarters in Bastogne. "But I agree it would be wise to withdraw them."

Unfortunately there was a brief disruption in the telephone line and Jones never heard the second sentence. Instead of ordering them to retreat, Jones left his men on the mountain.

At that same time, Middleton told another officer: "I just talked to Jones. I told him to pull his regiments off the Schnee Eifel."

This simple miscommunication sealed the fate of the 422nd and 423rd Regiments, as well as five artillery battalions. Roddie and the soldiers of the Golden Lions held their ground, even though the enemy was closing in from both sides.

It was a catastrophic mistake.

There was utter confusion and chaos. Behind the front lines, the roads were jammed with traffic fleeing in the opposite direction. "It was a case of every dog for himself," one major said. "The most perfect traffic jam I have ever seen."

The Americans never had a chance. As Roddie later wrote, what good were rifles against tanks and 88s?

Skip Friedman was on guard duty the first day of the attack. He was already suffering the effects of the snow and damp; as he marched at his post, his combat boots leaked, and he stomped his feet constantly to keep his toes from going numb. Only a few months earlier, he'd been in uniform on the University of Alabama campus, studying thermo-dynamics, calculus, and mechanical engineering. Now he was trying to fend off frostbite and trench foot, and to avoid being blown to bits by the Nazis.

The night of the attack, Skip entered the headquarters of the regimental commander and saw a detailed map hanging on the wall. "There are arrows north of us, south of us, and *behind* us," Skip said. He looked at the map and realized they were in trouble—and he didn't see a way out.

13
SURROUNDED

By the following day, Sunday, December 17, the German trap was snapping on Roddie and the two forward regiments of the 106th Division. At dusk, about nine thousand US soldiers were surrounded on the snowy German moor. They were in a dire position.

"None of us knew how serious the situation had become," Lester said. "I discovered it quite by accident on the night of the seventeenth when I walked into the command post and found the clerks quietly burning papers and documents. The next day I was told to burn all our communication codes, that we were slipping out of town to try to break through to our lines. That was [the] first indication I had that we were surrounded and cut off from our supplies."

In the morning, the atrocities began. Before 6:00 a.m., German soldiers entered the town of Honsfeld, where they found exhausted American soldiers sleeping wherever they could. Joachim Peiper, veteran of various Russian massacres, rounded up eight defenseless men, who were captured in their underwear and bare feet. They shouted "I surrender!" but he murdered them with a machine gun. Nine more attempted to surrender; all were brutally killed.

On the same day, the all-black troops of the 333rd Field Artillery Battalion were stationed just behind the front lines. Many of them were killed in the fighting; the others were captured by the Germans. As the men were being moved to the rear, an American aircraft attacked. During the confusion, eleven black soldiers escaped into the snowy woods and became lost.

The eleven men trudged through waist-deep snow, ultimately finding the tiny Belgian farming village of Wereth shortly before dusk. They waved a white flag, and a friendly farmer offered them food and shelter. Like many tiny towns in the region, Wereth was divided in its loyalties. The wife of a German soldier notified the Germans of their whereabouts, who then captured them at the home where they were hiding. The Germans tortured and murdered the men. The news of the savage torture-killings of the "Wereth 11" became known as the worst atrocity committed by Nazi troops against US forces during World War II.

This wasn't the only murder. Around noon, a tank regiment approached the town of Malmédy. An American convoy of about thirty vehicles arrived at the same time. The tanks opened fire, hitting the first and last trucks, setting them ablaze. Dozens of soldiers jumped off the trucks and ran into the forest. The Germans rounded up as many men as they could catch. Instead of taking them as prisoners of war, they were herded into a field by the road. The Germans took their rings, cigarettes, watches, and gloves, then eighty-four American soldiers were shot with machine guns. This mass murder became known as the "Malmédy Massacre."

Later in the afternoon, an American patrol discovered the first survivors of the massacre. Some soldiers came out of hiding and asked for help. Eventually, forty-three survivors were located.

Almost immediately, rumors that the enemy was killing prisoners reached the front lines. Shock and fury were widespread. The American command issued an urgent warning to all troops: "It is dangerous at any time to surrender to German tank crews, and especially so to tanks unaccompanied by infantry, or to surrender to any units making a rapid advance. These units have few means for handling prisoners and a solution used is merely to kill the prisoners."

German generals being held as prisoners of war in England were horrified at the news of the massacre. "What utter madness to shoot down defenseless men?" one said. "All it means is that the Americans will take reprisals on our boys."

Roddie and his men heard about the Malmédy Massacre. The troops knew that any American soldier—regardless of race or religion—was liable to be shot by the Nazis if he surrendered. That news strengthened the will of the American soldiers to fight harder, refusing to surrender.

They were running out of ammunition, food, and fuel, but Roddie and his men fought on. They had no choice.

That night, Roddie wrote in his journal: "I enjoyed my last hot meal on the evening of the 17th because the morning of—"

14
CAPTURED

Even though it appeared that the Allies would win the war, the bloody fighting continued. Hitler and his Nazi forces were more desperate than ever. On December 18, Sonny Fox and his men in the Twenty-Eighth Infantry Division surrendered. "Out we came, with our hands raised high," Sonny said, describing how his men left the few houses they still held in the tiny town of Hosingen. "My emotions were wildly mixed. Relief at being alive, fear of what was about to befall us, but also a keen curiosity about what this new experience would be like. I was curious to walk through the looking glass and see the German side of the war."

He was part of an organized surrender. When he left the house, he saw that the Germans had tanks and artillery aimed at the houses. "They were about to level us," Sonny said. "We had no choice but to surrender."

The men were forced to march toward the original

German front, where other men from his division were assembling. Nearly 7,500 men had been captured, in the largest mass surrender of the war. These were the opening days of what was to become known as the Battle of the Bulge.

That same morning in the town of Clervaux, Luxembourg, Technician Fifth Grade Paul Stern was camped out at the railway station with other men in his outfit of the 110th Regiment, Twenty-Eighth Division. Although they had been fighting for two days, all was quiet. They had no idea that the German troops were nearby. The Germans came up through the woods secretly, and before Paul knew it, the Americans were surrounded and captured.

As he was captured, Paul wondered what to do with his military dog tags. His name was Stern; he had Jewish features; the tags were marked with an *H* for Hebrew.

What would happen to a Jewish American soldier in Nazi hands? Paul spoke fluent German, and he had heard about the Nazi brutality against Jews. He hadn't had time to speak with the other Jews in his group. He would have to make up his own mind about what to do.

Paul slipped the dog tags from around his neck, smashed them with the butt of his rifle, and buried them in the muddy earth.

There were about 140 men captured with Paul, mostly

medics. After disarming the soldiers and stripping them of their valuables, the Nazis marched them into the lobby of the nearby Clervaux Hotel. They stood in their wet and muddy combat boots on the hardwood floor and wine-colored carpets, waiting to find out what their German captors had in store.

Paul thought about his parents back in the South Bronx. He worried about how his mother would take the news that he was captured or missing in action. He wondered how his brother, Jack, was faring in France. It had only been a few weeks, but it now seemed so long ago that he had marched in a parade to celebrate the liberation of Paris and the promise of an end to the war.

After waiting for about ten hours in the hotel lobby, a German soldier stormed in, holding a pistol in a black-gloved hand. He asked for someone who spoke German. Even though he was fluent in German, Paul had promised himself that he would not speak it. He didn't want to be used by the Nazis or to assist as a translator.

Paul looked straight ahead. "The SS man walked over to me and stuck the pistol in my chest," Paul said. "Of all the people in the place, he looked toward me. I wondered who'd ratted me out."

With the weapon leveled at his back, the German soldier led Paul into a nearby room.

"What do you want?" Paul asked in English.

They wanted Paul to tell the leader of the American forces in Clervaux to surrender.

Paul said he was not an officer.

"Who's your officer?"

Paul led them straight to his superior officer, a man Stern and his buddies did not trust or like. Before capture, the officer had been stealing drugs from the dispensary. Paul told them, in German, that this was the unit's commanding officer and that he should be the one ordering the surrender.

The German soldier pointed his pistol at the major. He would have to be the one to give the bad news.

On the morning of December 18, the 422nd Regiment moved from the village of Schlausenbach to a rendezvous point in the Ardennes. While the rest of his regiment pulled out—including Roddie, Skip, and Frankie—Lester Tannenbaum stayed behind to rig an army jeep to serve as a "dummy radio station." The goal was to trick the Germans into thinking the Americans weren't abandoning their position entirely.

Lester worried that his was a "casualty assignment," one that put him at increased risk of death because he was exposed and defenseless in the city after everyone else had left. Two other men—Bossi and Jones—had volunteered to stay behind with him. The men worked fast, so they were able to pull out just before the German soldiers arrived.

The 422nd had hoped to rejoin its sister regiment, the 423rd. When they arrived at the predesignated crossroads, clothing and equipment were scattered in the snow as far as the eye could see. To Lester, it was obvious that everyone in the 423rd had stripped down to fighting essentials and thrown away anything that might restrict movement and maneuvering.

Lester's men rummaged through the snow, picking up items that could be of use. Lester had a jeep, and he loaded it with overcoats, sleeping bags, and chocolate bars. It had been three days since they'd had a proper meal, so the chocolate was welcome. Roddie, Lester, Frankie, and Skip sat at the crossroads, waiting for the regimental commander to decide on their next move.

The men had a chance to talk for the first time since the fighting had begun. It was a losing fight and they all knew it. Just nine days earlier, they had been carefree. Now they had seen death, and they knew what combat was really like. They also knew fear, but they didn't talk about it. Instead, they talked about scruffy beards and furloughs to Indianapolis and girls they'd met in England.

After a few hours, Lester, Roddie, Skip, and the other men in the convoy started to imagine getting safely back behind Allied lines. And then Roddie received word from command. "We're going to attack," Roddie told his men. "We go at dawn."

At first light, the soldiers left from the three battalions would launch an assault on Schönberg, a city that was now behind enemy lines. At the same time, another division planned to attack from the opposite direction. The goal was to punch through the German lines at the same time, creating an escape path for the surviving members of the 106th.

Because Roddie and the other men in the convoy were already in the dense woods around the town, they were ordered to maintain radio contact within the regiment.

During the night, they took up positions in the dense woods. It was risky to move through the German-occupied area, and they all prayed for an overcast night with no moonlight to give them away.

Slowly the convoy moved out. Lester wondered how the drivers managed without headlights. It was so dark that they couldn't see the jeep in front of them. To prevent one jeep from ramming the next, a soldier in the back seat would hold up his phosphorescent watch to indicate distance. It was like a trail of fireflies through the forest.

The convoy reached the heart of the woods without encountering the Nazis. It was the middle of the night and pitch-black when they piled out of the jeeps and started digging their foxholes. The ground was frozen and snow-covered, so it took longer than usual.

As soon as Lester finished his dugout and crawled into his sleeping bag, the firing began. Bullets whizzed around them. It was too dark to see anything, but Lester could recognize by sound the difference between German and American forces' gunfire.

The fighting stopped as quickly as it had started. Lester later learned that a small German patrol had stumbled into their perimeter. The Germans had been driven back, but there was no more rest that night. Lester, Roddie, Frankie, and Skip waited in their holes, wondering what tomorrow would bring.

The fighting started again with the dawn. The morning of the nineteenth, Roddie and Lester got the first view of their new position. They had to sit tight and wait until they received word about how the other battalions were progressing. At about 8:00 a.m., a courier arrived, letting them know the Ninth Armored Division had been held back by fierce German resistance. Their plan was doomed.

The other battalions of the 422nd who had engaged at Schönberg had walked into a death trap. Their weapons weren't as powerful, and they soon ran out of ammunition. They were slaughtered: almost every soldier involved in the attack was killed or captured.

A group of soldiers spotted a Nazi armored battalion approaching. The remaining officers of the 422nd joined the 424th, which they hoped was still holding its position at the town of Bleialf. They were told to abandon all equipment that wasn't necessary for fighting their way out. Roddie and his men had guarded the precious equipment they were now going to blow up to keep it out of enemy hands.

Roddie sent out their last radio message: "Destroying equipment." When they finished, the convoy started out of the woods. As soon as they hit an open stretch, the Germans began to fire on them. When one of the jeeps was hit with shrapnel, they abandoned the jeeps and ran for cover. This turned out to be a good defensive spot. Still, Roddie and Lester knew the odds were against them.

Roddie watched a group of soldiers run toward the woods. They were cut down by machine-gun bursts as they ran through the snow. Lester and Roddie had discussed their chances of reaching the American lines if they could escape into the forest. The machine-gun fire changed their minds.

The men were ordered back into their vehicles. They revved the engines and made a dash for safety. Another part of the convoy remained behind to try to hold off the Germans. German troops fired on the jeeps and trucks as they made their way up the steep hill, as the retreating American soldiers threw gear and ammunition out of the vehicle in an attempt to lighten the load. All Roddie, Lester, Skip, Frankie, and the other soldiers wanted was to escape so that they could live to fight another day.

* * *

As the German troops approached, they made false promises in English, booming through their loudspeakers: "Showers, warm beds, and hotcakes!"

A single tank rumbled down the road. For a moment the men thought they might have armored support, but when they stepped outside, the Nazi crewmen inside the captured tank opened fire on the Americans. All hopes of rescue were dashed.

By mid-afternoon, Colonel George Descheneaux, commanding officer of the 422nd, could see the writing on the wall. He had two thousand men, ready to make a last stand.

How many soldiers would the Germans take prisoner?

How many would they shoot in cold blood?

"We're still sitting like fish in a pond," said the commanding officer. "I'm going to save as many men as I can, and I don't give a damn if I'm court-martialed."

The men were to blow up their jeeps and destroy their remaining weapons so that the Germans couldn't use them. The major knotted together two white handkerchiefs and approached the Nazi troops.

The battalions were outgunned, outnumbered, and surrounded. Roddie, Lester, Frankie, Skip, and some other soldiers of the 422nd followed the colonel's orders to try to punch through the Nazi lines and escape. The soldiers jumped back into their trucks and headed south. It was a furious and confused scramble. Several trucks were stuck in the mud; some overturned. The rest got away.

The Germans were everywhere.

Roddie was behind the wheel of a jeep, and he spotted his buddy Sergeant Jack Sherman knee-deep in the snow. "Jump in, Sherman!" Roddie shouted. "We're bringing up the rear." He hit the gas, and their jeep sped off, the last vehicle in the convoy.

Sherman was a wisecracking Jewish kid from Rochester, New York. Though small and wiry, he was a tough, stand-up guy and one of the regiment's best-trained soldiers. Roddie was glad to have Jack riding shotgun.

Twenty vehicles barreled through the ice and mud. The gravel road was rutted, filled with slush, and the tires of Roddie's jeep kept skidding. After clearing several hills, Roddie heard a loud explosion as the lead jeep was hurled into the air. It had hit a land mine.

Roddie and Jack screeched to a stop. A number of soldiers were badly injured.

As they tended to the wounded, German artillerymen locked in on their position. Everyone ran, taking cover in the trees along the slope. From their elevated position, Lester and Roddie could see tanks and infantry advancing. It was impossible to escape. All Roddie and the others could do was keep low and return fire with their rifles and pistols.

German troops emerged from the forest. Most wore white uniforms and capes, camouflaging them perfectly in the misty and icy forest. Roddie, Lester, Frankie, Skip, and Jack were surrounded by hundreds of Germans. They could also see other Americans being captured in the distance.

Should they be killed or surrender? The captain who was with them ordered the men to destroy their rifles. Roddie loved his weapon. "I knew [it] as I knew my clothes, or anything else," he wrote in his journal, but he "couldn't bear the thought of some German using it." That image of a German using it to kill other Americans hardened his resolve.

With sadness, Roddie destroyed the firing pin, then smashed his rifle against a thick pine tree. Reluctantly, Roddie threw away his pistol, spare ammunition clips, hand grenades, wire cutters, and compass.

Again, the Jewish soldiers had to decide whether to rip off their dog tags and bury them in the deep snow. Some swapped dog tags with those around the necks of the dead Americans. Lester destroyed his dog tags before he destroyed his rifle. Skip Friedman kept his tags around his neck. "When we were captured, many of the Jewish POWs threw away their tags," Skip said. "I was really a little pessimistic about what was going to happen to us—so I decided to hold on to my dog tags so [my body] could be identified."

As each group of soldiers surrendered, the Germans searched the prisoners for valuables and stripped them of their overshoes and winter coats.

There was shouting between a Nazi lieutenant and a

sergeant. "Hank, what're they saying?" Roddie whispered.

Technician Fourth Grade Hank Freedman, raised in an Orthodox Jewish family in Boston, was listening carefully. He spoke Yiddish, a language with grammar and vocabulary based on medieval German. Hank could make out most of the conversation.

"They're debating what the hell to do with us," Hank said.

The German sergeant was eager to get going. Rather than taking the Americans as prisoners, he wanted to shoot them all. "We can't waste time with these vermin," he said. "Let's shoot them and go!"

Roddie watched the enemy lieutenant's face closely. He knew that his life and the lives of all the men in his company hung in the balance. If the German officer ordered execution, he and his men would do everything in their power to stay alive.

For his part, as a man of deep faith, Roddie had every intention of surviving.

In those short December days, it was already dark at 6:00 p.m. It was a bitter-cold, snowy, windy night. The Germans ordered their prisoners to lie down.

"Sleep in the snow!" came the order.

The captured Americans were forced to lie in a muddy, frozen churchyard. "Come on," Roddie said to Jack Sherman.

"Let's try to get some sleep." They huddled together to keep warm. All night, captured American soldiers joined Roddie and his men. Few thought they would make it until morning. Besides freezing to death, the worry of every soldier was that the Germans might suddenly decide to fire on them with machine guns. The atrocity at Malmédy had been committed not so far from this churchyard. The fear of a sudden burst of machine guns never left their minds throughout the night.

15
MARCH

At dawn on December 20, the Nazis shouted for the POWs to get up and begin marching. In the stark winter daylight, Roddie and Jack got a full understanding of the destruction around them. All the American jeeps and tanks were burned. They saw the dead bodies of their fellow 106th Division brothers twisted and frozen. These were friends—guys who'd been with them in training, guys who had laughed, joked, and talked about their families.

Every mile or so Roddie heard a blast from a Nazi rifle. That was the fate that awaited anyone who rested, walked too slowly, or tried to escape.

The Nazis forced the prisoners to march, with no regard for their well-being. "We were lined up, stripped of all but clothing, and marched off. What a sad, disappointed, sorry lot we were," said John Morse of the 423rd Regiment. "Helping the wounded along, we merged with other new POWs to form a ragged phalanx of shuffling zombies."

They marched for miles without food or water. Roddie and a few other men managed to grab some sugar beets along the side of the road. They ate a bit and handed the rest to the shivering soldier next to him. Some risked their lives to bend over and cup their hands in puddles of dirty water to drink. If a Nazi guard saw an American drink, he'd hit him or threaten to shoot.

Many of the troops suffered from numbness and pain, especially in their feet. Roddie developed frostbite in his toes, but slowing down wasn't an option.

Soldiers helped each other keep up, because falling out was fatal. "If you didn't march, you didn't last," said Skip.

They continued past German tanks, artillery, and thousands of enemy soldiers moving to the front to push toward Antwerp. "German troops moving up to battle would stop some GIs to search for watches and other souvenirs," said Morse. "Our combat boots attracted a lot of attention. A German would place his boot next to a GI's and, if the size looked right, demand a swap."

As they went through a town, a civilian in a business suit ran up and hit one of the soldiers in the head with his briefcase. The German guard said that the man was upset over the recent Allied bombings.

Not every German guard was equally brutal. Some Germans were career military and others had been drafted. In either case, they knew they had to go along with the plan or they'd be shot by their own officers. Skip said, "As we were marching, this regular German soldier comes up to me—he spoke good English; it turns out he had lived in New Jersey—and he said: 'You guys are lucky. Your war is over. We've got to go on until we get wiped out.' He was right."

Rumors spread through the ranks. Roddie heard they were being marched to a railway hub, which could only mean they were being taken deeper into Nazi territory.

"We were marched 31 miles without food and water," Roddie wrote. "We were herded into a lot and slept or lay in the mud until morning. We were then given two bags of hardtack, the most distasteful crackers I have ever tasted, also some cheese. This was the 21st of December. Our first food."

The men of the 106th and Twenty-Eighth divisions were mixed together. That night, they again slept huddled together for warmth. Roddie realized that there would be no relief, no rescue any time soon. "We would remain as captives of our enemy," another soldier said. "Life would go on until God or the Germans decided to end it."

16
INSIDE THE BOXCARS

On the morning of the twenty-first of December, after eating the distasteful crackers and cheese, the order came for Roddie and the men to form ranks and march into the Gerolstein railyard. Vicious dogs barked at them as they were herded into boxcars headed deeper into Germany. Each boxcar was designed to hold four horses, or perhaps thirty men, but was now crammed with sixty POWs or more. The men had to stand because there was no room to sit or lie down. Many of the men were wounded or suffered from trench foot and frostbite. "The boxcars turned out to be the same type of boxcars that were taking the Jews to concentration camps," Sonny Fox said.

The boxcars were mostly dark, the only light inside coming from four tiny openings covered with barbed wire, two on each side at the top. According to the Geneva convention, a group of treaties that set standards of how prisoners should be treated during war, the boxcars should have been painted with "POW" signs to help Allied pilots distinguish them from enemy trains. To not do so was a war crime. But the Germans did not mark the cars carrying the American soldiers.

The sanitary conditions inside the boxcars were appalling. The boxcars were filled with hay and covered with urine and animal excrement. Soldiers had to relieve themselves against the wooden walls, or sometimes right where they stood. Many of the GIs suffered from dysentery and diarrhea. The men used their steel helmets as toilets, then tried to dump the contents out through the small openings above them. The stench of urine and feces was overpowering. They were living in filth.

Roddie tried to maintain discipline, but the cramped and nasty conditions made it next to impossible. They had no water or food, and they did not know where they were going.

Some of the prisoners told stories. "We kept telling stories that made us laugh," Lester said. "It's the thing that kept us going even though we were starving. We'd be talking to each other about our experiences—not so much about combat, but what life was like back home. That's what we were living for."

For the prisoners, the trains moved agonizingly slowly, sometimes pulling off the main tracks and stopping for minutes or hours at a time. They had to pull aside whenever a

German military train needed to pass.

Once, while the train filled with the POWs waited, a train carrying German soldiers stopped on the next track. The American troops didn't want to show their desperation. Instead of showing fear, they traded insults in English and German, most not understanding the words their enemy yelled.

One week after the Ardennes counteroffensive began, the bad weather that had served the German army so well during the initial days of the battle gave way to bright blue skies. Now the British and American airmen could fly reconnaissance and bombing missions. The Allies sent relief to the troops still fighting in Belgium. The Royal Air Force sent three thousand bombers to destroy industrial and military targets in Germany.

Roddie was most likely thinking of Christmases back in Tennessee, walking with friends and family to the Methodist church just a few blocks away from home. The church, a small redbrick building that to Roddie's young eyes—as he recalled in his diary—resembled a castle, would be as dark and lifeless as the boxcar. But it slowly would come to life, glowing with a blaze of candles and the joyous sounds of carols. Young Roddie loved singing in unison with his father and aunt, brothers, and cousins.

Silent night. Holy night.

The image was suddenly shattered by the buzz of Royal Air Force planes coming in low. Instead of greeting the sound with whoops of joy, the men locked in the boxcars shouted in terror. Because the trains had not been marked on the roof as carrying POWs, they were now the targets.

As they stood in the boxcars, they heard a hissing sound and light flashed through the barbed-wire slits in the boxcars. Flares dropped from the planes and lit up the railyard as if it were daytime, guiding the way for the heavy bombers to unleash their loads.

Fifty-two British fighter-bombers were high above with bombs to level the railyard. Next to the boxcars filled with POWs were railcars loaded with Nazi heavy artillery.

Panic started with the first explosion. Another blast. Closer. This time a direct strike on one of the forward cars.

The men heard the screams from their fellow soldiers as some of the boxcars derailed and burst into flames. A few men were able to escape. Some ran from the wreckage only to be shot down by the guards or killed by concussions from the blasts.

The soldiers trapped inside the boxcars were powerless. "You can't run, you can't hide," said Sonny Fox. "In combat at least you can move, dig in, seek cover, or shoot back. To be sitting there, listening to the bombs coming down, with no alternative but to wait and hope each one missed—that seemed to make the word 'hopeless' totally inadequate."

In Roddie's boxcar, men clawed at one another and tried to rip through the wood with their bare hands, desperate to escape. Some of the prisoners tried to break through the barbed-wire-covered vents with their bare hands, bloodying their fists.

"From the other side of the boxcar I heard a voice with a southern drawl rise up above the noise and chaos," Hank Freedman said. "It was Roddie." His commanding voice focused the attention of the panicking troops. "Roddie said very calmly, 'Boys, if you have ever prayed to God, you need to pray now and ask him for salvation. Have faith! God will save us. Pray, boys, pray!'" The men quieted and prayed.

Hank was astonished at the transformation in the car when Roddie bowed his head and prayed aloud.

Their prayers were answered: the bombing slowed. The men heard the screaming of the dying, and there were occasional blasts from Nazi rifles, but the thunder and tremors of the bombing eventually stopped.

Roddie's boys astonished him with their bravery. He was proud: they had obeyed his commands even in the face of death.

17
CHRISTMAS 1944

After the bombing, the men remained locked in the boxcars until the next night. They were traumatized, thirsty, and hungry—but relieved they were still alive. Without warning, the door of the boxcar opened. A German guard threw a loaf of bread inside. "Merry Christmas," he said in English with a heavy German accent.

It was black bread, made with sawdust filler, and smaller than a typical American loaf.

How were they going to share one loaf among sixty starving men? They turned to Roddie, who was the ranking officer. Roddie carefully tore the bread into sixty pieces, each no larger than a pat of butter.

After the food was distributed, Roddie began singing "Silent Night." A second soldier joined. Then a third.

The guards shouted something in German and banged their rifle butts against the door to quiet them.

The POWs silenced.

"To hell with them," shouted one of the soldiers. "It's Christmas Eve!" He began singing with as much gusto as he could. In no time, the entire boxcar was singing again.

It was a moment of rebellion. At the end of the song, they fell silent again, having shown their independence.

A few moments later, they heard several soldiers singing "Silent Night" in German.

Stille Nacht! Heilige Nacht!

Alles schläft. Einsam wacht.

Some of the soldiers sang the Christmas carols they remembered, and they were echoed by their captors with the German versions. "The words were different but the songs—and maybe the emotions—were the same," Morse said. "For a few brief hours there was peace on earth among us there in a ruined freight yard."

But for Lester Tannenbaum, he cringed when he heard the Nazi troops singing "*O Tannenbaum, o Tannenbaum, wie treu sind deine Blätter!*" He knew that *Tannenbaum* meant "fir tree" in German. The classic Christmas carol had a new and terrible association with his name. Lester vowed that if he survived, he would change his name when he returned to New York.

On Christmas Day, after four days locked in the boxcars, the trains finally stopped in a small town. The door flew open and the men were ordered out. Roddie, Lester, Frankie, Hank, Skip, and the other soldiers fell out of the trains, their limbs freezing, barely able to stand. They were filthy, their uniforms fouled from the dirt of the battlefield, blood, and excrement.

The train had stopped before the depot so that the men would be forced to march into the town known as Bad Orb. The word *bad* meant "spa" in German, and the town featured several hot springs that were said to have curative properties. It was also the site of Nazi Germany's largest prisoner of war camps, located several miles up a nearby mountain.

One of the soldiers remembered looking at the scene around them—green pines, outlined against the blue sky and fresh white snow. "Look around," he said. "If I weren't so cold, so hungry, and so scared, this would be one of the most beautiful places I have ever seen."

The beauty reminded Roddie of the Smoky Mountains back home.

Roddie and the other POWs made a difficult five-mile hike from the train station up a steep, zigzagging icy mountain pass. As they marched, some of the soldiers cupped their hands and filled their mouths with snow to try to quench their thirst.

Eventually, they arrived at Stalag IXB, where most of them would remain for the next month. Originally a World War I army training camp, the massive facility became known for having some of the most unsanitary, disease-infested conditions of any Nazi POW camp.

Most of the wooden barracks had broken windows. The camp latrine was an open pit, about six feet square, surrounded by low poles on short supports the men were expected to balance on while using the facility. "The Nazis' goal," Skip said, "was our humiliation."

They were formed up into ranks for the five-man count so the Germans could begin their first official documentation of imprisonment. Roddie and most of the others understood that this was necessary; it was the only way their families could be notified that they were not killed in action but rather POWs in Germany.

18
THE POW CAMP

In German camps, prisoners were divided by branch of service and rank. There were camps for enlisted men and noncommissioned officers and separate officers' camps for commissioned officers. Life as a POW was different for officers and enlisted men. Specifically, officers weren't obligated to work as prisoners.

Roddie and most of the other soldiers had committed to memory their legal protections. The War Department had issued a pamphlet titled, *If You Should Be Captured, These Are Your Rights.* "When you are questioned," the pamphlet instructed, "by [any] enemy authority, you must give only your name, rank, and serial number. Beyond that, there is no information which the enemy can legally force from you. Do not discuss military matters of any sort with anyone."

When they arrived, POWs were forced to fill out two information cards, one for the International Red Cross and another for German military records. The German captors issued the men identification numbers with dog tags and asked them to fill out questionnaires with personal information. "One of the first things they did was to ask us our whole family history, what our family name was, where we came from, the names and address of our relatives and things of that nature," Hank Freedman recalled. "Of course, we didn't tell them. We said, 'Here is my name, this is my rank, and this is my serial number and that's all you're going to get.'"

Roddie, Frankie, and Hank were among the group of twenty soldiers who flat out refused to tell the Germans any additional information. As a consequence, the Germans ordered them to strip to the waist and stand outside in the brutal cold for more than an hour and a half. They shivered, rubbed their hands on their arms and shoulders, and stamped their feet to try to delay the onset of frostbite.

An American officer who saw what was happening told them to tell the Germans what they wanted to know. "Look, guys," he said. "It's ridiculous for you to persist in not giving them the information."

Roddie didn't agree with the officer's decision, but he also didn't want to see the other soldiers suffer needlessly.

Beyond details of family life and addresses, the Germans demanded one other piece of information for their files: *religion*.

This, of course, was a problem for Jewish soldiers.

Lester, Skip, Paul, Sonny, and Hank weighed the decision carefully. Should they proudly say, "I am a Jew"? Should they trust they would still be treated as United States soldiers, even in Nazi captivity?

Those who had destroyed their dog tags or swapped with a dead soldier had the chance to deceive the Germans. Lester told his captors he was Presbyterian. "Very few of the Jewish prisoners identified themselves as Jews," Lester said. "We were too smart for that."

Sonny Fox recalled getting to the front of a line and encountering an American POW designated by the Germans to assist with the registration process.

"Name?"

"Irwin Fox."

"Rank?"

"Sergeant."

"Serial number?"

"42022375."

"Father's name?"

"I'm only supposed to give name, rank, and serial number."

"Listen, kid, if you don't answer these questions, they're going to make you stand in the snow until you do."

Simply wanting to get out of the cold, Sonny figured that the Nazis were "not going to win the war" if he gave them his father's name.

"Julius Fox," Sonny said.

"Occupation?"

"Textile converter."

"Religion?"

At first Sonny refused to give an answer.

"Religion?" The clerk was waiting impatiently.

"Jewish."

The clerk looked up from the form, stared at Sonny for a moment, and said, "Protestant."

At first, Sonny thought he had misheard him.

"Jewish," he repeated.

Then, finally, Sonny understood what was going on. He was a Jew in Germany. Why place himself in peril? The clerk was trying to protect him.

But Sonny wouldn't change his answer. He had already surrendered and thrown down his rifle. He didn't want to renounce his faith. He refused to surrender morally.

"Jewish," he repeated.

This time the clerk didn't even look up.

"Protestant!" he said, waving Sonny away. He wasn't about to waste any more time on some fool who didn't appreciate what he was trying to do for him. He told Sonny to move on, and he did.

Inside the camp, the barracks were badly overcrowded. Most housed up to one hundred men. Broken windows allowed the bitter cold into the building. There were three-tier bunks, some just wooden slats without bedding. The few available mattresses were pads filled with dried grass and ferns. The men had no blankets, and there was no heat. The soldiers had only their field jackets, no overcoats, gloves, or hats. Despite these conditions, the exhausted men collapsed wherever they could find a space.

Skip thought the conditions were part of the Germans' overall strategy to dehumanize the POWs and turn them into animals. Staff Sergeant Earl Verham, a medic in the Twenty-Eighth Division, recalled what a chaplain at Bad Orb had told him: "It isn't what happens to a man that matters. It's how a man reacts when something happens to him that matters." In the camp, individuals proved themselves as animal or man.

The POWs developed their own system of justice. A makeshift court listened to evidence and pronounced a sentence; they kept a written record to turn over to American officials when they were freed. "If a slice of bread was stolen, the sentence would be one week of latrine duty and a recommendation for reduction of rank when liberated," Verham said.

Simple gestures helped keep the men sane. For Frankie, it was washing out his undershirt, socks, and pants to feel at least somewhat clean. Sonny took the advice of an older POW in the barracks, who told him to shave and to wash his socks. "I respected this man and decided to do it," Sonny said.

There was a single razor blade for 240 men. There was only a cold-water tap in the latrine. "To shave meant that I had to stand there, in the freezing weather, in the cold outhouse, shaving with a dull razor," Frankie said. "But I had committed myself to doing it. It took about twenty minutes, and every time I cut a follicle, it brought tears to my eyes. By the time I finished shaving, my hands were frozen, my fingers about to fall off. But I did it."

The simple acts of humanity made Sonny feel more like himself. "I had taken back control of my life," he said. "Yes, I was still a prisoner, but in some very important place inside of me the barbed wire had come down. I had learned that even under the most hopeless of circumstances, one does not have to be helpless. I learned another valuable lesson through this experience—man cannot exist without a social structure." Sonny had learned the social structure of the military, one based on rank.

In the first few weeks at camp, there was no recognizable social order. "Gradually, a new structure valid for this peculiar situation emerged." Power came from skills—knowing how to speak German, how to give a haircut, or how to tailor a pair of pants gave a man authority.

The soldiers watched one another grow weaker day by day. Their skin grayed, hair dulled, eyes became vacant. No one needed a mirror; all he had to do was look into the gaunt faces of those around him.

They received only starvation rations. "Our daily diet consisted of breakfast—ersatz [fake] tea with no sugar whatsoever, dinner 3/4 of a litre of inedible soup. Supper 1/6 of a loaf of bread and approximately 1 1/2 square of potato margarine," Frankie wrote in his journal.

At 6:00 a.m. the barracks lights came on and the guard shouted, "*Raus! Raus!*" "Get out! Get out!" Once the men were accounted for, each group dispatched a two-man team to the canteen to fetch the morning "coffee," which was actually just dark roasted grains of some sort. "The only good thing one can say on behalf of this brew is that it was warm," recalled one POW.

There were no dishes or cutlery, so men often received their "coffee" and soup in their helmets. The coffee and "grass soup" had nearly no caloric value. The main meal was a small portion of black bread that some soldiers described as more like a paving block than anything edible. Most of the soldiers received only five to six hundred calories a day.

Lester later wrote that his most vivid image of camp life was the way that the men cut that black brick loaf between six men. "That small loaf of what the Germans called bread, our meager daily ration, was our only solid food," Lester said. "It tasted mostly of sawdust. Six men shared one loaf and we took turns in cutting it, with that person being the last to choose from the six pieces." Some men ate their piece quickly; others saved some for later. Some men traded their bread for a cigarette or two.

Other groups developed elaborate rituals to decide who got the bread. "The ceremony of the bread took longer than the actual consuming of the slice," Sonny said. The process of cutting, choosing, and of course consuming that tiny portion of sawdust bread was a highlight of most POWs' days.

Frankie described the ritual in his journal. "Louie, myself, Paul (a new and good friend) and Roddie had coffee every night with our bread. It's really something to watch us when we get our bread. We cut it up into small paper-thin squares and toast it on top of a small stove we have in the orderly room. We look forward every day to our night together when we toast our meager supper and chat about home, our loved ones and food."

Every once in a while, a fight would break out, but the men were so weak that few fights resulted in fisticuffs. "A friend and I got into a violent shouting match one day over some real or imagined insult," one soldier wrote. "We decided to settle it outside." It wasn't long before they realized fighting was useless. "The effort to swing was too great, even if we landed a blow it would be ineffective. We fell into each other's arms laughing at our ridiculous behavior."

To keep the men occupied throughout their days of captivity, some of the sergeants organized religious groups and educational programs. Anything to take the men's minds off their ever-present hunger. Frankie recalled finding solace in daily prayer, religious services with other POWs, and taking time to read Roddie's Bible.

Roddie prayed and read scripture daily, mostly in solitude. "I want peace, quiet, and more than anything I want God," he wrote in his journal.

"Faith was something that you could rely on because . . . [the Germans] did everything that they could do to break me down physically," recalled artilleryman Corporal Russell Gunvalson of the 590th Field Artillery Battalion. "But the only thing I had left was my faith in God. That's one thing they couldn't take away. As a matter of fact, I think it probably made me stronger. It taught me that life is precious and you need something. You can't go through life alone. You've got to have somebody there that you can confide in."

Heightening the misery of the starvation rations was the infestation of lice, bedbugs, and other vermin in the barracks. All the men suffered these infestations. Beyond the painful bites and scratching, the POWs learned the lice could transmit pyrexia, also known as trench fever. In severe cases, the infected lice bites could cause death. Eventually, the Nazis became concerned by the health risks and ordered a general delousing.

Master Sergeant Roddie Edmonds,
1940s

Staff Sergeant Frank Cerenzia,
1940s

Sergeant Sonny Fox,
1940s

Staff Sergeant Lester Tanner,
1940s

Unidentified soldiers completing the Infiltration Course, Camp Atterbury, Indiana, 1943–44

Lester Tanner

Roddie Edmonds

Roddie Edmonds, Frankie Cerenzia, Lester Tanner, and unidentified officers, 422nd HQ Company, Camp Atterbury, Indiana, 1944

Unidentified town, Battle of the Bulge,
December 1944–January 1945

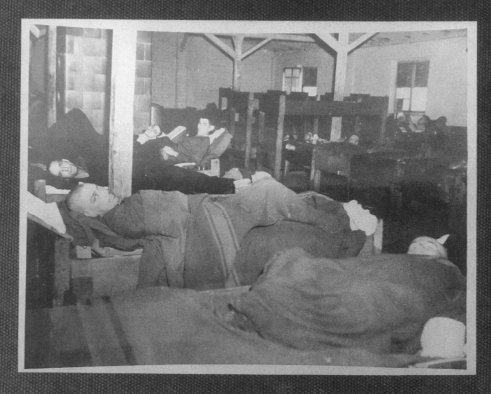

Unidentified American POWs, German stalag,
1945

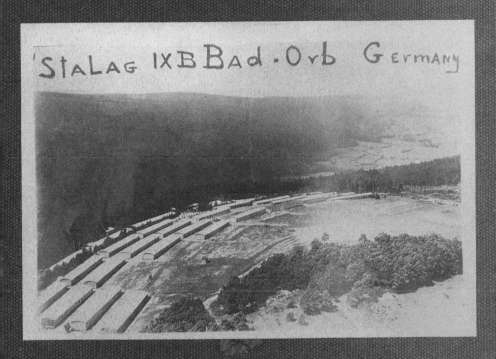

Roddie's first POW camp, Stalag IXB Bad Orb,
Germany, 1940s

"Wednesday, we were 'deloused,'" Frankie wrote in his journal. "We were given baths and our clothes were steamed for approximately 1/2 hour. The bath in itself was useless as we had no soap. But it was pleasant to have our bodies under hot water for a change. That was the day I first noticed how rapidly my weight has been leaving me."

In a war crimes investigation conducted in 1945, many soldiers recounted numerous cases of dysentery brought on by the malnutrition and poor hygiene. The medical supplies were woefully inadequate. They had some first-aid kits with a few aspirin and crepe paper for bandages.

For men who smoked, cigarettes were often a more valuable commodity than food. Throughout the day, men could be heard calling out, "Bread for cigarettes! Bread for cigarettes!"

Frankie traded his watch for a loaf of bread and two pounds of potatoes and one pound of beet sugar. He sold a portion of the food to Roddie and some other men. He didn't keep the money long. "The craving for cigarettes became so bad that I began to buy them at the fantastic price of $10.00 per cigarette," Frankie said.

Roddie had hidden his US cash in his shoulder patch. He pulled it out and spent it on cigarettes for Frankie and other friends who were starting to grow desperate.

19
SEPARATING THE JEWS

Three weeks after they arrived at the POW camp, the Americans were told to separate into two groups: Jews and non-Jews. All Jews had to identify themselves by six the next morning. Any Jews found in the barracks after this time would be shot. The Americans banded together and refused to permit the Jewish soldiers to obey the order. "We protested that we were all Americans and wanted to be treated equally," one of the soldiers said. "But we were told it was a direct order from the high command."

Indeed, according to a 1944 report made by a Swiss delegate of the International Red Cross, a Major Siegmann is listed as the "Accompanying Officer from the High Command."

The Oberkommando der Wehrmacht (OKW)—high command of the German Armed Forces—headed by Field Marshal Wilhelm Keitel and General Alfred Jodl—insisted on a policy to segregate Jewish POWs from non-Jewish POWs. This was in keeping with the overall Nazi policy of anti-Semitic persecution. Visiting delegates from various nations observed this religious segregation firsthand and offered considerable testimony about it after World War II.

Pierre Arnaud, one delegate for the French government, wrote, "We as the delegates always protested [the separation of the Jewish POWs]" into special barracks, or work details, called *kommandos* by the Germans. "Our argument was that the Jewish prisoners were soldiers, like anyone else."

Arnaud testified that the Germans were "obsessed with race," even in the treatment of captured Allied POWs. Following an official visit to a prison camp in northern Germany, he wrote: "I found myself by chance in a barrack where the Nazis had put the Jews and the [Catholic] priests—two groups that were considered by the Germans as the fiercest enemies of Nazism."

Major Siegmann—acting with the full weight of the high command—reacted with characteristic harshness and anger to the Jewish American POWs' defiance of the first order. He shortly issued a second order, threatening that "all Jewish violators," when caught, would be summarily shot and that other GIs sheltering the Jews in their barracks would also be executed. The Jewish soldiers met among themselves and decided to obey rather than risk the lives of other prisoners.

Lester, Paul, Skip, and Hank were among the group of Jewish soldiers to identify themselves. Along with other self-identified Jews, they were moved to barracks surrounded by barbed wire. Lester called it "a prison within the prison." There were soldiers of all ranks—enlisted and officers together—jammed into the unheated barracks.

No one knew what lay in store for the Jewish GIs. The segregation of the men seemed to shock them speechless. It was almost too brazen and chilling to discuss.

Roddie tersely described the event in his journal: "January 18, 1945—Jewish moved out."

Though many Jewish soldiers had already identified themselves, the Germans knew there were more Jews among their captives.

Sonny Fox remembered the Germans reading out a list of Jewish prisoners at roll call, causing him to wrestle with his identity. "That's a moral crisis for a nineteen-year-old. Do I remain mute, or do I say, 'Take me! I'm Jewish'?" Sonny asked. "Finally, I rationalized that if I was going to help [the other Jews] at all, it would be easier to help them from outside than inside."

That night, Sonny—the supposed "Protestant" sergeant from Brooklyn—was shocked by the anti-Semitic jokes being told in the barracks by the American soldiers. "It was one of those moments where you think about the distance between who we profess we are as a people and who we really are as individuals in society," he recalled.

After a few days, another Jewish soldier, Ernest Kinoy, decided he couldn't live with the guilt of pretending to be Christian while other Jewish GIs were being segregated. "I knew a number of people who were down there in the barracks," Kinoy said. "I went and turned myself in. Basically, it was an ethical decision. . . . Of course, the possibility of the Germans doing something was apparent, because you don't segregate without something in mind."

On January 24, 1945, a delegate from the International Red Cross visited the camp. He found the conditions unacceptable: in addition to overcrowding, the men were sleeping on bare floors, without blankets or adequate heating. They had learned of multiple deaths from diseases among the POWs.

The official report from the Red Cross stated: "The Delegate . . . told the Camp Commander that in his opinion, the present accommodation was untenable. In reply, the Camp Commander claimed that this is only a transit camp and that the prisoners would be transferred elsewhere at the earliest possible opportunity." When the Red Cross pressed the issue, the Nazi commander said that he planned to transfer the men the following day.

Soon after, a supervisor from a slave labor camp arrived to take 350 more prisoners for a "special work detail." The

Nazis could take POWs under the rank of noncommissioned officers for forced labor. The German leaders knew that there were more Jews who had not identified themselves within the American POWs, and they were determined to find them.

At dawn on January 25, the camp commandant ordered all of the noncommissioned officers—about 1,300 men, both Jews and non-Jews—to stand in formation in knee-deep snow and howling wind. After more than four hours of standing in the frigid condition, the men were marched downhill back toward the Bad Orb train station. Most of the men limped along on frozen feet.

The men were each given one-third of a loaf of the black sawdust bread and one-third of a can of beef, then told they were bound for a new camp. "In spite of the bitter cold and our frostbitten feet, our spirits were much higher," Frankie wrote in his journal. "We had hope of better food and some long-prayed for Red Cross packages."

They marched two hours back to the Bad Orb train station and were again placed in boxcars. They traveled 170 kilometers (100 miles) northwest, to Stalag IXA, a POW camp in Ziegenhain, a small town in central Germany, arriving midafternoon.

When the doors of their boxcars opened, Roddie saw that they had arrived at a small railroad yard with multiple tracks that had been recently bombed by the Allies. On the way from the station, they faced fierce blizzard conditions. Wind whipped across the barren fields. Most men kept their heads down, tucked into their jacket collars, keeping their gaze on the boots of the GI marching in front of them.

Roddie and the other POWs had been surviving for more than a month on less than five hundred calories per day. Their physical deterioration in those weeks of captivity was startling. They wore the same clothes in which they had been captured. They were infested with lice and stricken with dysentery. Most suffered from frostbite and trench foot.

The German guards had no mercy. Throughout the grueling march, they shouted for the men not to fall behind or slow their pace at the risk of a gunshot.

Inside the gates of the camp, the men were forced to stand in formation for hours while large German shepherds growled at them. Eventually, two German guards brought forward a young Russian POW, about eighteen or nineteen years old. He was gaunt, like he was on the verge of starvation, unshaved, and wild-eyed.

"You're free to go," the commandant said.

The Russian POW, knowing there must be a trick, refused to move.

The guards opened the gates. The Russian POW had no choice. With rifles pointed in his direction, he took a few cautious steps toward freedom—then started running toward the gate.

The commandant made a hand signal. The gates suddenly closed, and the dogs were unleashed. Within seconds, the young prisoner was mauled to death. At last the boy's screams stopped.

"Remember this well," Commandant Mangelsdorf said. "If any one of you disobeys orders, the same fate awaits you."

Roddie's journal entry that day was a single word: "Dogs."

20
HATRED AND LOVE

Paul Stern couldn't stop thinking about the Russian kid he had just seen brutally murdered or the boy he had seen without a face.

Back in the early hours of the fighting in the Ardennes, on the afternoon of December 16, Paul had been scrambling among the bodies of the wounded, the dying, and the dead. He had rushed to the side of a young GI who had stepped on a German mine and was severely injured. The soldier was only nineteen years old, just like Paul.

Paul tried his best to treat him, but it seemed futile. He had never felt so powerless as a combat medic. All Paul could do was sprinkle a little sulfanilamide on the wounds.

Bobby was the boy's name. Paul was sure he hadn't lived more than a day. Paul had prayed for him and had gotten him evacuated to the rear lines, but . . . that picture stayed in his mind, haunting him throughout his nights in Stalag IXA.

A day never went by when Paul didn't think about Bobby.

And a day never went by when he didn't think about the young lieutenant and the other soldiers standing by a pillbox in the Siegfried Line.

Paul learned an important lesson on the day he was approached by a frightened young lieutenant who asked for help when they were still on the battlefield back in the Ardennes. "Stern," he said, "you've been around quite a bit. I don't know a thing about combat. What do I do?"

Paul wasn't sure what to say. "Sir, all I can tell you is to keep your butt as close to the ground as possible and pray like hell," he said. "That's the only thing you can do when you're under fire, sir."

Soon after, Paul saw the lieutenant and two others standing near the entrance to a German bunker. They were smoking cigarettes and talking, completely exposed. Paul knew that there were Germans inside the bunker, so he sprinted over and pulled the men out of harm's way.

Suddenly, a German soldier inside the bunker opened a slit in the door and tossed out a hand grenade, which exploded in the spot where the lieutenant and soldiers had been standing. They recoiled from the blast, unhurt behind a concrete wall. Because of Paul's actions, they had been saved.

After they returned to camp, the lieutenant told Paul's commanding officer about the incident. The next morning,

Paul was promoted from private to corporal. He also received the Bronze Star for heroism.

Lying in the barracks, Paul fully grasped what had happened at that German pillbox. He had saved three men's lives, and by doing so, they might have indirectly saved his. Now that he was at Stalag IXA with the other noncommissioned officers, he had escaped whatever fate awaited the Jewish privates back at Bad Orb. Paul acted because he considered it the right thing to do, but he appreciated the consequence. "Whenever you help people," he often said later, "you help yourself."

Paul and Skip formed a special bond while POWs. They continually lifted each other's spirits, even as they were starving. Paul promised Skip that they would be free men by Passover that spring. "He assured me we would be eating matzo by Passover," Skip said. Paul was a man of faith. He'd witnessed several miraculous episodes during his time in Europe. In the days before the horrific Battle of Hürtgen Forest, in late October 1944, Paul had been one of the team of men who captured the ancient city of Aachen, the first German city to fall to the Allies.

On October 29, Paul had gathered with more than fifty other Jewish soldiers from various combat units to conduct Jewish services on Rosh Hashanah, the Jewish New Year. Several of the men draped their shoulders with prayer shawls; others, like Paul, remained in full combat gear, bowing their heads in prayer while still wearing their steel helmets. The service took place near an old Jewish cemetery by the German line. Radio microphones and cameras captured the servicemen singing and reciting Hebrew prayers on the battlefield.

The fighting was so close that, as they prayed, the Jewish GIs could hear artillery shells exploding. The Rosh Hashanah service was broadcast the next day on the NBC radio network throughout America. Later, the service was broadcast into Nazi Germany. It was the first time, since the rise of Hitler, that Hebrew prayers had been heard over German airwaves.

The day after the ceremony, Paul had returned to the cemetery with a Jewish American lieutenant. In a large tomb they found hundreds of rare Jewish religious books and Torahs, which they assumed had been placed there by Jewish leaders for safekeeping before the synagogue was set on fire. Many of the books were eight or nine hundred years old.

Paul worried that the books might be destroyed in the shelling. He took the books to a Roman Catholic church and monastery and asked the Mother Superior if she would hide the books in the church.

"If the Nazis ever come back," she said in a whisper, "they will cut all of our heads off." But the Mother Superior was brave; she said, "Yes."

It took Paul and the lieutenant half a day, but they managed to safely hide the sacred ancient Torahs and prayer books in the church.

In the barracks at Stalag IXA, Paul was suffering, like all the other men, from the effects of starvation. But he never lost faith. He told Skip over and over that he was certain they would survive. "Skip," Paul vowed, "we're going to celebrate Passover as free men."

Still, even as he entertained thoughts about his life as a free man, he couldn't escape the image of Bobby or his increasing concern about the Jewish soldiers left behind at Bad Orb.

Back at Bad Orb, the Germans were intent on finding 350 Americans for a work detail. They gathered soldiers with "Jewish-sounding" surnames, as well as those with "Jewish-looking" faces. They filled out the group with non-Jewish "troublemakers" and "undesirables," such as Private First Class Johann Carl Friedrich Kasten.

When the Germans pressed for the names of remaining Jewish soldiers, Kasten protested. He was fluent in German and had visited prewar Nazi Germany as a teenager, but Kasten was a patriotic American who had enlisted in the army in 1943. Kasten was taken to a second-floor conference room, where several German officers were waiting.

"There were eight chairs and in front of one of the chairs was a loaf of bread, very obviously a bribe for something coming," Kasten said.

He took his seat and the senior German officer said, "Kasten, we want the names of all the Jews in the American camp."

Without any hesitation Kasten pushed the loaf of bread to the center of the table. "We are all Americans," he said. "We don't differentiate by religion."

Kasten was jerked out of his chair and thrown down a flight of stairs. He lay in the street and after he determined nothing was broken, he returned to his barracks. He shared his story and urged everyone to deny being Jewish.

"Something is bound to happen and soon, and none of the men should admit to being Jewish."

That afternoon, the Germans ordered the entire camp—about four thousand American servicemen—out on the parade ground. The commandant stood on a small platform and shouted, "All Jews, one step forward!"

Because of Kasten's warning, no one stepped forward. "This infuriated the officer to an extent that he jumped down from his platform, grabbed a rifle from one of the guards, and rushed towards me," Kasten said. "I was convinced he was going to shoot me, but instead, holding the barrel, he swung the rifle like Babe Ruth and with all his strength crashed the butt against my chest. I flew backwards about fifteen feet and fell on the ground. I couldn't breathe. I thought I was done for."

While Kasten lay there dazed, the guards went through the ranks of men and pulled out any GIs who "looked Jewish." Kasten was ordered to join them.

The soldiers were force-marched to Bad Orb, crammed into boxcars, and taken on a four-day odyssey by train—with no food or water—to a concentration camp in a town called Berga. Kasten was again named a leader. The slave labor detail—made up mostly of political prisoners and European Jews from concentration camps—was part of an "emergency fuel program" to transfer synthetic oil production deep underground in order to protect it from Allied bombing. The top secret project included a massive construction zone of seventeen different tunnels and a large factory area. Everything in Berga was under the supervision of fearsome SS soldiers.

In freezing and inhumane conditions, Kasten and the Berga slaves blasted and hacked out tunnels, while inhaling dangerous dust that left most of them with lung problems. At the concentration camp, they faced constant mistreatment, starvation, and beatings.

Their only meal was a weak soup and a tiny portion of "bread" containing sawdust, ground grass, and sand. The European Jewish workers were killed for minor infractions, or at the whims of the Germans.

"The agony of it all soon became evident," Kasten wrote. "We had to get up while it was still dark, march to the mines to dig the tunnels without food or water and 12 hours breathing stone dust and hauling out carts loaded with stone. Very soon after arrival, the men started dying of exhaustion, malnutrition, and extremely harsh treatment."

Seven days a week, the POWs excavated rocks and dirt by hand and shovel after it was loosened by the explosives. They pushed carts filled with rocks to an area where they could be dumped into a nearby river. They worked with primitive drills and old mining machines; the men were used in place of machines or horses to move heavy objects.

Fatal accidents and brutal beatings by the guards were commonplace. Soldiers deteriorated and many lost their will to live.

Many of the overseers were older men who were used as a last resort. They proved to be just as barbaric as any Nazi. "Beating the prisoners, hitting them with the butts of their rifles, were spontaneous expressions of their own individual bestial acts against mankind," said one soldier.

The POWs at Berga expected to die. Most seemed to accept it; others remained unbreakable, such as Kasten. Undaunted by the brutality, Kasten wrote that he requested a meeting with Lieutenant Willie Hack, the SS officer in charge, and pointed out that he would someday have to answer for his actions.

Hack's answer was blunt: "You were brought here to work and that's what you will do!" He read aloud Kasten's identification tags: *Johann Carl Friedrich Kasten*.

"You are a German and you have come here to destroy the Third Reich," the commander said. "You know, Kasten, there is only one thing worse than a Jew. Do you know what that is?'"

Kasten remained silent.

"It's a traitor who betrays his country. And you are a traitor."

The horrors of slave labor in Berga would continue for weeks, even as it was clear to the Nazis that the war was lost. It was the only POW camp in which American soldiers experienced brutality similar to Nazi concentration and death camps. Of the three hundred and fifty POWs sent to work at Berga, seventy-three died in the ten weeks. The fatality rate at Berga would prove to be the highest of any camp where American POWs were held during World War II.

21
STANDING TOGETHER

It was dark by the time Roddie and the rest of the men saw their new prison barracks on January 25. Stalag IXA, near Ziegenhain, was a sprawling camp divided into categories by nationality—French, British, Serbians, Soviet, and now American.

As a master sergeant, Roddie was the top-ranking American infantryman in the camp. He had the most seniority because he had enlisted in the peacetime 1941 army. But it was also evident to the other corporals and sergeants that he knew how to look out for their best interests. "Roddie by now was our barracks leader," Frankie wrote in his journal. "He got the job because he knew how to give good commands and he was a good soldier."

Skip considered Roddie "a very stoic guy, very solid." Roddie was considered tough but fair. "He would take no garbage from anybody—particularly Germans," Skip said.

"We were very lucky to have him with us."

In the camp there were five American barracks, each holding between two hundred and fifty and three hundred men. The overcrowding wasn't as bad as it had been at the previous camp, but the building was still dirty, dark, freezing cold, and infested with vermin—barely habitable. It had a cold-water tap, but no toilet in the barracks. Each man had only a thin blanket, so the men huddled together for warmth. They crowded into the triple-tiered bunks, sleeping on thin burlap-sack mattresses filled with straw. Two or three men shared each narrow bunk to keep from freezing during the night.

The next morning, January 26, a major arrived at the camp. Word quickly spread that it was Major Siegmann, from the Oberkommando der Wehrmacht—the German army's high command—who had separated the Jewish Americans from non-Jewish soldiers at Bad Orb.

That afternoon, the camp loudspeakers announced in German and then English:

> *Tomorrow morning at roll call, all Jewish American prisoners must report to the Appelplatz* [the place where roll call was performed], *only the Jewish Americans—no one else. Anyone who disobeys this order will be shot.*

"These were the same orders we'd received at Bad Orb," Lester recalled. "Only this time, we were organized. Roddie, for the first time in this experience, was in complete command. There was no one there to give him orders. It was his decision."

Roddie said, "We're not doing that. Tomorrow morning we all fall out just as we do every morning."

Frankie knew that Roddie would never comply with an illegal and immoral order—he was too good a soldier and too decisive a leader—but how could Roddie defy the Germans without putting everyone's lives at risk?

Roddie sat quietly, probably in prayer, and most likely recalling favorite Bible passages like Romans 8:37: *Yet in all these things we are more than conquerors . . .*

The fate of 1,292 malnourished, frostbitten Americans depended on him.

Roddie's plan was simple, but risky. He called a meeting of leaders from the other barracks. Several of the most senior sergeants gathered around Roddie's bunk as other men stood as lookouts at the door and windows.

He ordered that every infantryman assemble in military formation in the Appelplatz as part of the standard 6:00 a.m. roll call. Roddie stressed that everyone must follow his order to defy the Nazis—all 1,292 Americans in camp. He further stressed that even the men too sick and too weak to walk could not be left behind in the barracks.

On January 27, at precisely 6:00 a.m., there was a sudden banging on the barracks doors. The men hustled outside.

The hard-packed snow crunched under their shuffling boots. Roddie glanced back to see if *all* the men were following.

The men assembled as planned. Even the sick did their best to stand up straight in formation. A few were having trouble, leaning heavily on the shoulders of other POWs—but they formed up in ranks.

Roddie had faith in God and he trusted his men. He knew that his men wouldn't voluntarily betray their brothers-in-arms. But what if starvation and desperation weakened their resolve? What if a single man decided to save his own skin by pointing out the Jews in the ranks? What if the plan didn't work? He shook off the doubt and gathered his resolve.

Suddenly, a Nazi officer approached the plaza. He scanned the ranks of the men standing in formation. What was this? A joke? He expected a couple hundred Jewish soldiers. He did not expect to see all 1,292 American POWs.

It was Major Siegmann.

The major belonged to an old military family. He had served in World War I as a professional career officer. After World War I, he saw the social troubles in Germany and was disgusted by the German government (the Weimar Republic) so much so that he left Germany and moved to the United States, where he rose through the ranks of General Motors as an executive.

When World War II started in Europe, Siegmann

tendered his resignation from General Motors and left his life in the United States. He returned to Germany to volunteer for service in the Wehrmacht (German army) out of a sense of patriotism. Siegmann, very angry at the United States, held extreme nationalistic German views, and was a true believer in the Nazi cause.

As the overall head of the Prisoner of War section of the Wehrmacht high command, Major Siegmann was essentially the eyes and ears of Hitler in the camps, particularly during the frequent visits of delegations that came to check on the treatment of POWs. He reported directly to Field Marshal Keitel and General Jodl, both of whom were eventually convicted of war crimes at the Nuremberg trials and executed by hanging.

Major Siegmann was described by one delegate of the Vichy French government as "a very tough and very hard man. When he said 'yes' it was 'yes.' When he said 'no' it was 'no.'"

The major bolted toward Roddie and shouted, "What's this?"

Roddie held his strict posture, jaw fixed, looking straight ahead.

"Under Article Seventeen of the Geneva convention," Roddie said, "prisoners of war are only required to provide name, rank, and serial number."

The major approached to within striking distance of Roddie.

"Don't quote regulations to me. Were my orders not *clear*, Sergeant? Only the Jews were to fall out."

"We will give you name, rank, and serial number," Roddie said. "That's all."

"Only the Jews!" Siegmann shouted. "They cannot all be Jews."

Roddie turned and met the Nazi's eyes. "We are all Jews here," he said.

Roddie's bravery unified the troops and spread throughout the ranks. Hearing their leader's calm resolve emboldened the soldiers. Not a single soldier broke ranks, faltered, or flinched.

Enraged, the major pulled his pistol from its holster and lunged forward. He pressed the gun barrel hard into Roddie's forehead, right between the eyes. "Sergeant, one last chance," he said. "You will order the Jews to step forward or I will shoot you right now."

There was an eternal silence. No words. No gestures. Only swirling gusts of snow and the smoke like puffs of the soldiers' frozen breath floating skyward.

Roddie could see Lester on his immediate left, and Paul on his right. Though they were both afraid, like Roddie, they kept up stoic expressions.

At last Roddie spoke. "Major, you can shoot me, but you'll have to kill *all* of us," he said. "Because we know who you are and you *will* be tried for war crimes when we win this war—and you will pay."

The major's hard face turned white; his arm trembled. His pistol was still pressed to Roddie's head—his finger still on the trigger.

Then, quickly, the Nazi pulled the pistol back, holstered it, turned, and fled the compound.

22
HUNGER

The men returned to the barracks after the showdown between Roddie and Major Siegmann. "We really cheered Roddie," Lester said. "He never wavered. What he did made us brave. He thought only of his men. That takes *courage*. But that was Roddie. We all came to admire and respect him. When Roddie said something while we were prisoners, that was what we did."

But Roddie didn't want to talk about what had happened.

Roddie also knew the danger wasn't over.

All the American POWs—both Jewish and non-Jewish—continued to face peril. Every day brought the risk of death—from freezing, starving, or being shot by the German guards for some minor infraction. Everyone continued to fear that an officer from high command would try again to remove the Jews.

Roddie felt the desperation of his men. He tried to restore a sense of military discipline to the POWs. Frankie wrote about the low morale among the prisoners. "Only a small handful have managed to hang on to their pride and self-respect," Frankie wrote. Many of the men had "stooped to everything but murder over a spoonful of soup or a crumb of bread. Stealing is simply terrible and if you manage to save anything for the next day, you've got to sleep on it in order to hang on to it that long. It's awful to see a once carefree and reckless American hunk of humanity stoop to a form of animal."

The men needed a new organization to curb their cut-throat survival-at-all-cost impulses. Each barracks contained about three hundred men, who divided themselves into groups of fifty, with one leader. Roddie remained in overall command. They created a staff and divided themselves up into several areas of responsibility: health, sanitation, food, discipline, and maintenance of the chain of command.

Even though they were POWs, they were still subject to military regulations. There were specific rules they had all been taught:

> *If I am captured, I remain a soldier. I am guided by the Code of Conduct and subject to the Uniform Code of Military Justice. I am entitled to protection under the provisions of the Geneva*

convention. . . . I will take no part in any action which might be harmful to my comrades. And more to this point—I will make every effort to escape and aid others to escape. I must be prepared to take advantage of escape opportunities whenever they arise. POWs must organize in a military manner under the senior person eligible for command and the senior person shall assume command. Strong leadership is essential to survival and noncommissioned officers will continue to carry out their responsibilities and exercise their authority in captivity.

In addition to getting organized, Roddie realized the men needed intellectual stimulation. "We were almost as bored as we were hungry," Sonny wrote. The men organized a camp lecture series, drawing on the skills and experiences of the men in camp. Speakers included a park ranger from Yellowstone National Park, an Ivy League professor, a newspaper editor, a Broadway producer, an architect, and someone who worked in the New York City district attorney's office and shared stories about mob activities.

The most popular speakers were men who knew how to cook, especially Johnny Barbeau, a chef from Dayton, Ohio. The men ate up every word as Johnny described his delicious menus and taught the men how to make their favorite dishes. "Recipes began to sound like poetry," said Sonny.

Some of the POWs listed their favorite foods in their journals. "We got so used to being hungry," Paul said. "Food was all we talked about. We listed all the foods we would eat if we could get back home."

Johnny and Roddie decided that they would open a new restaurant known as the Jolly Chef when they got home.

Roddie wrote in his journal:

> *Decided on restaurant business Thursday 15 Feb '45*
>
> *Definitely decided on restaurant business Friday 16 Feb '45*

A desperate man has a greater chance of staying alive if he has the hope of a future. They designed menus and floor plans. Planning the restaurant gave their lives a purpose.

The French POWs provided great support and assistance to the American POWs. They were better adapted to life in Nazi captivity, and they received monthly parcels from the International Red Cross in Geneva. "The French looked in good shape, physically, and were willing to give or lend some of their Red Cross parcels," said one of the POWs. The food in the packages kept the POWs alive.

The standard Red Cross issue was "one per man, per month." But the American POWs never received any during their time in the camp at Ziegenhain. They welcomed anything the French were willing to share. "We received our first Red Cross package today," Frankie wrote in his journal on February 8. "Although it was a one-man box, we had to share four men to a box. But what a joy. Inside was 5 packages of smokes, a 2 pound can of Oleo margarine, 2 cans of sardines, a box of prunes, box of biscuits, a full can of cocoa, a can of good coffee, a can of powdered milk, sugar, jelly, meat, cheese, etc."

The French also shared news from the front lines. The French POWs had managed to rig a radio. They listened to news from the BBC—the British Broadcasting Corporation—then relayed the information to an American who spoke French. That person then spread the news to spokesmen for each of the five barracks, who told the news to everyone else.

"At six o'clock at night, we would put someone at the door so that if a German guard was coming in I could switch to a lecture on something innocuous," said Sonny. "Then I would, by memory, describe what was happening on the Western and the Eastern fronts."

Only through the reports on the BBC did the American POWs learn that the Battle of the Bulge had been an enormously costly victory for the Allies, and that even though the men had been captured and were behind barbed wire, they'd played a crucial role in stopping Hitler's drive toward Belgium.

Some of the newscasts were difficult to hear. One particularly grim broadcast came on January 28, 1945. The day before, the Soviet Union had liberated Auschwitz in Poland, the Nazis' biggest concentration camp. The reporters said that hundreds of thousands of Polish people, as well as Jews from a number of other European countries, had been held prisoner there in appalling conditions, and many had been killed in the gas chambers. The details were staggering, even more so because it was the same day Roddie had risked his life by standing up to the German major.

When they weren't following the news reports, the POWs tried to stay alive and stay sane. The ongoing malnutrition changed their bodies and minds in unexpected ways. "Starvation reduces the functions of the male glands and enhances those that are more female-like," Sonny wrote. "Men's facial hair turned softer and their voices went up in pitch."

In early March, the POWs were joined by a medical officer named Captain Stanley E. Morgan. Originally from New Orleans, Captain Morgan had been a POW for six months when he was transferred to Stalag IXA. An Army Air Forces officer in the 101st Airborne Division, Morgan didn't live in the barracks with the noncommissioned officers but was a welcomed addition to the camp leadership.

"Captain Morgan answered medical questions that were on the minds of all of us," POW Pete Frampton recalled. "Things like, 'How long can we keep going on rations like these?' . . . Six months of this would be about the limit. The poor guy didn't have any medicine to offer us, but he encouraged us in many other ways."

The men suffered from jaundice and full-blown

starvation. They faced psychological problems: some had given up all hope of liberation and were just waiting to die. They were slowly drifting away, somewhere between daydreams, sleep, and death. Some considered suicide.

Roddie knew that once a man lost the will to live, he was doomed. He ordered that the most energetic men—those he called his *up* guys—tend to those nearest death—the *down* guys. He had the strong help the weak. The *up* guys helped the *down* guys to get to their feet each morning, to walk until the blood circulated through their freezing legs, to eat whatever food was offered, to think of home—their parents, sisters, brothers, girlfriends—and to visualize the day when the Nazi criminals would face stern justice.

Receiving news from the front was so vitally important that Roddie ordered the Americans to build their own radio. As a communications chief, Roddie felt certain he could help his men put one together if they had the right parts. "The radio we had in the POW camp was put together by the radiomen who had been trained by the army for that job," Lester said. It was made from parts smuggled into the camp by the POW volunteers who worked in the town of Ziegenhain. The component parts for the radio had to be brought into the camp, reassembled, and hidden during barrack inspections by the guards.

Once it was completed, the radio allowed the troops to directly monitor what was going on in the war. "Feb. 23,

1945 was a big day for us," Frankie wrote in his journal. "We had been patiently looking forward to the Allies starting their big drive in the West to cross the Rhine and begin the final phase of the war. Today it happened. The big drive had finally started and was meeting with success. Now everyone was in high spirits again."

Men regularly gathered around the makeshift radio to track updates about General George Patton. They listened to reports of Patton's effort to move through the same terrain where Roddie and the 106th Division had fought. They listened to news that Patton's forces had reached and crossed the Rhine River.

Roddie and the other POWs celebrated Patton's seemingly unstoppable momentum. "We've learned that Gen. George Patton has captured 70,000 Germans, Cologne has fallen, the Rhine has been crossed in a number of places," Frankie wrote in his journal. "At night and all day, we can very clearly hear the battle sounds of artillery. Our boys are not over 85 miles away from here. Every single day we can see or hear thousands of our planes flying into the very heart of Germany and laying many noisy eggs. By April 5th I expect to be eating good army chow till I burst, and by the middle of May I expect the most hated nation in the world to be crushed completely. I hope and pray I'm right."

23
HOPE

Day by day, the Allied bombing got closer, giving all the POWs hope of freedom. As the front grew closer, the high point of the men's day became watching the contrails of the B-17s as they made their way toward Germany on their daily bombing runs. "Sometimes," Sonny wrote, "there would be hundreds of them and the deep, pulsating noise of their four engines was the affirmation that the war was moving into its noisy final stages."

"This armada of American power was a tremendous boost to our morale," Sonny said.

The men liked to harass the guards by singing their own rewritten version of the "Battle Hymn of the Republic."

We're a bunch of Yankee soldiers living deep in Germany
We eat black bread, a little soup, and a beverage they call tea

And we have got to stay right here till Patton sets us free
And we go rolling home—
Come and get us, Georgie Patton
Come and get us, Georgie Patton
Come and get us, Georgie Patton
And we go rolling home

By the middle of March, the sounds of the Allied air attacks grew so close that the entire camp shook. "For the past 24 hours there has been terrific bombardments very close to us," Frankie wrote in his journal on March 19. "It hasn't stopped once. I'm inclined to think that something big is up. I sure hope I'm right."

On March 21, the first day of spring, most of the men were outside in the sunshine, watching the Allied planes in the distance. In the middle of the afternoon, they saw a squadron of US Army Air Corps fighters, which accompanied bombers. The POWs knew that on the way home, the P-47 Thunderbolts were cleared to attack any targets of opportunity. They worried that their camp looked quite a bit like a German army barracks.

On the first pass, the POWs out in the compound waved to the pilots.

Then a German guard shot at the aircraft with his machine gun.

The fighter swooped down suddenly, firing at the camp with its six wing-mounted .50-caliber guns. The bullets tore through both the French and American compounds, sending men scattering and diving for cover.

"We were lucky," Sonny said. "We were digging slugs out of the wooden bunks for days."

The damage in the French compound was far worse. Eleven French POWs were killed and forty-nine injured. "As we watched the bodies being borne past our compound, the sadness was accentuated by the realization that after five years as POWs, they had been killed by their ally as liberation was at hand," Sonny wrote.

The unexpected attack left the men in a state of shock and high anxiety. It might not be the last attack. Could they come all this way, survive the battles, the forced marches, the Christmas Eve bombing, the starvation, only to die by the friendly fire of their own air force's planes? The men knew it was only a matter of time until American forces would reach them, but would they survive long enough to see freedom?

The POWs worried that the camp would be bombed again, and some demanded action. They wanted to paint "POW" on the barracks roofs, but the commandant refused to allow it. On March 24, American bombers hit a little town just outside of camp. There were also rumors that before the

Allies would be able to reach them, the Germans would force-march the prisoners—now numbering approximately sixteen thousand—deeper into Germany.

Rather than wait, a small group of soldiers held a meeting and decided to try to break someone out so the Allies could know about the POW camp. Three men volunteered to try to break out.

On March 29, about 1:00 a.m., the three POWs tried to escape and make their way to a group of American troops posted about seventeen miles away. The details of the escape are unclear; accounts differ, but what is known is that the effort proved to be fatal. African American Sam Harris was shot and left in a trench until he bled to death. According to POW reports, he was killed before he made it out of the compound by a cruel German sergeant known as "Hook Nose." An English medical officer concluded from his examination of the body that Harris had been murdered.

The senseless murder of Sam Harris had a chilling impact on the entire camp, leaving many men frightened, angry, and determined to exact justice.

The POWs went through a long and thorough count. The guards forced the prisoners out of the barracks into an empty field in the usual five-man columns. They counted and recounted the men for hours.

According to some, the Germans threatened reprisals if anyone else tried to escape.

"Two guards carried our dead hero's body back and forth in front of us while the camp commandant lectured us on the futility of trying to escape," POW John Morse wrote. "One more attempt and six men from the guilty party's barracks would be executed." It wasn't a risk anyone wanted to accept.

24
FREEDOM

As the expectation of freedom grew, so did the POWs' apprehension and fear. The Americans sang about General Patton coming to their rescue, but they weren't sure that they would live to see the general's tanks and jeeps barreling through the camp gates. By that point, most of the POWs had lost fifty to eighty pounds. It wasn't clear how many more days they could survive under such conditions.

"Things are finally beginning to look up and I hope and pray we're free men soon," Frankie wrote in his journal. "This is the most horrible experience I've ever had in my life. Five men died in the last 24 hours from starvation and that doesn't make me feel any better either."

The men worried that the Germans might try to move them out of the camp before they were liberated. Frankie wrote about his anxiety in his journal.

March 26. Today is a tense day. . . . Something is up and none of us know what it is. Frankly, I'm worried. Some Germans are already leaving the camp.

March 27. Our armies are only 35 kilometers away and swiftly moving closer. . . . Something is happening all right and unless they should move us out, we'll be free by Easter. That's what I'm so darn worried about. They can move us and if they do, we're all sunk until the war's over.

March 28. What a day. This morning, I received the good news that the allies are only about 15 miles away. Then what I'm most fearing has happened. We were told we would be moved out tomorrow.

Roddie, medical officer Captain Morgan, and the other camp leaders knew that a march would prove fatal to many of the men, who were not strong enough to keep up. In addition, once they left camp, it would be difficult to identify them as POWs. "It was important that we not leave the POW camp because once outside you were subject to being shot by your own planes, which were everywhere," Roddie wrote.

Roddie knew that the German plan to evacuate the camp broke the Geneva convention's rules by placing the prisoners in danger. He also was aware—thanks to the BBC news broadcasts—that as Germany faced inevitable defeat, the Nazis were force-marching tens of thousands of men—from prisoner-of-war camps, work camps, and concentration camps—deeper and deeper into the heart of Germany. In addition, he had heard that the POWs who were too sick or weak to march might be left behind to die.

"The Great March, as we called it, was to begin at sunrise the next morning," one of the POWs said. "We seldom spoke of death in the camp. Perhaps none thought we would die there because we had escaped death in combat. This changed when we were ordered out on the roads. Then, I thought we would all die."

Frankie's journal also includes a dark notation. "I wrote a letter to Lucy for Louie to take back. It sounds more or less like a last will and testament. Who knows? Maybe it is."

He wasn't the only POW to think he was in his final days. Many soldiers wrote what they thought were the final letters to their families, prepared their wills, and tried to make peace with God.

Again, Roddie refused to give in to defeat. Liberation was near. He would not allow the men under his command to comply with the Nazi order to march. "We're just too weak to go on a long march," he told Lester.

Once again, Roddie came up with a plan. And, just like his last plan, when he told all his men to stand together and claim to be Jews, this plan carried considerable risk.

His plan: defiance. "No one marches out of the camp," he said. "No one."

When the order came to fall out, Roddie told the American POWs that they should do anything to stay in camp—delay, hide, pretend to be too ill to march—anything to stay in the camp. Every third man was ordered to fake sickness and fall to the ground. The men to the left and right of the fallen would help him back into the barracks. Perhaps by delaying the count and stalling, by dropping to the muddy ground in agony, they could prevent the German attempt to evacuate the camp.

The danger came from the confusion. If the guards became angry or confused, then they might fire on the troops in frustration. Still, Roddie didn't have a better plan. He wanted to find a way to stay at camp as long as possible since the American troops were only days from reaching them.

All the POWs were scared. Few could sleep as the morning roll call approached.

At 6:00 a.m., the Germans called for the POWs to line up.

As Roddie had ordered, no one moved from his bunks.

The Germans ordered them to get moving.

At 6:15, the men were still in the barracks. Guards burst in with snarling German shepherds. The dogs snapped at the POWs and the Germans shouted in anger.

"We moved out in a rush, trying to avoid the sharp teeth

of the big animals," one POW said.

Roddie had ordered as many men as possible to hide. Some climbed underneath the barracks; others hid in the latrines. This frustrated the Germans in their five-man count.

As the Americans formed slowly into ranks, they saw the French marching out of the camp.

When the order came to march, the Americans moved only a few paces before GIs started to collapse in apparent pain. The guards moved up and down the ranks, screaming and kicking those on the ground. The dogs growled and barked. Some of the men were bitten.

Roddie and the rest of the men continued to carry the supposedly sick men into the barracks. In no time, every American was back inside. "We spent about half the day playing sick," Frankie wrote, "and all this time Patton was drawing closer and closer."

But *playing* sick wasn't enough. As the Germans grew more impatient, Roddie ordered the POWs to make themselves ill.

"After we came out of hiding and were assembled, I told all our people to eat grass and dirt and get sick," Roddie wrote. "I told them not to fake it but to really get sick. They got so sick one of the German guards cried. Half of our people were sick and the other half carried them back into the barracks."

Some men swallowed soap to foam at the mouth.

Others pretended to have convulsions.

Many continued to roll on the ground, moaning and muttering incoherently.

Captain Morgan even prepared a concoction from supplies in the infirmary that made several of the soldiers vomit.

Roddie wanted to make the Germans believe his men had a ghastly—and perhaps contagious—disease.

Next, the Americans watched the Germans march the British soldiers out of camp.

Then the Russians.

Then the Serbs.

Every time the American soldiers formed up, Roddie would give the order, "Break ranks!" and the men would fall to the ground or dash back to the barracks.

By now the Germans were getting furious at the Americans stalling. Some started firing their rifles into the air.

They ordered the Americans to send at least twenty men from each barracks out immediately.

After several hours, the exasperated commandant stood face-to-face with Roddie.

The Germans realized they had only a brief window of time before their own escape route out of Ziegenhain would be blocked. Patton's army was close. Tanks were closing down the roads.

"Finally the old German colonel came down and threw

up both hands and said we had won and could have the camp. He was leaving," Roddie wrote in his journal. "The Americans were the only group that were not marched out."

It was an incredible accomplishment. "[Roddie's] sense of duty, responsibility, and devotion to the soldiers under his command went far beyond his own personal safety," Paul Stern said. "All the American prisoners at the camp were saved due to his outstanding courage."

The German officers and guards left the camp. But the men were still at risk.

Roddie ordered that all the men go back into the barracks. They were told to stay away from the windows, to remain silent, and not to use any lights, fires, smoke, or cigarettes. If any German troops walking past saw that the Americans were still there, they would be killed. They went into hiding.

Some German SS soldiers arrived, but the Americans remained out of sight. Later, more SS soldiers arrived, followed by armored vehicles. The POWs were terrified that they would be spotted and then massacred like Sam Harris or the unarmed American prisoners at Malmédy.

Nearly 1,300 men remained silently hidden. After more than one hundred days in captivity, the POWs knew every corner of the camp and every possible hiding place.

Roddie's journal entry for the day ended with just a single word: "Hiding."

* * *

The German troops assumed the camp had been deserted, so they left, hurrying east into Germany, fleeing Patton's army.

The Americans posted their own guards around the camp to keep watch for other approaching troops and to prevent the men from losing control and looting. "We found that we owned the camp," Frankie wrote in his journal. "All the Germans had skipped out. . . . There was a tension in the air as thick as butter. Tension so great that hunger was forgotten."

The POWs expected the American forces to arrive at anytime. Every passing hour, the POWs could hear sounds of heavy American artillery getting nearer and nearer. They soon heard the sounds of rolling armor and tanks approaching. They could see houses in the town of Ziegenhain flying white flags of surrender.

At 3:30 p.m. on March 30, American tanks rolled down the road in Ziegenhain, turned at the guard tower, and entered the camp. One tank broke through the camp fence, not waiting for the gate to be opened. It was Patton's Sixth Armored Division. Paul Stern recalled that as the American armor rolled in, "the boys ran to the fence, kissing the tanks."

To the ragged, starving POWs, Patton's men, in their

clean infantry uniforms, "looked like giants." Sonny stared at the American troops. "Man, are they *fat*," he said. At his starvation weight of 104 pounds, he was used to seeing nothing but skeletal soldiers in sagging, filthy olive-drab uniforms.

"Chaos broke loose in the camp," Frankie wrote in his journal. "All prisoners busted out of their compounds and greeted Johnny Doughboy with hugs and kisses and genuine tears of joy." He called the moment the Americans arrived "the greatest thrill of my life."

The POWs scrambled onto the roofs of the tanks, yelling and cheering.

Patton's men were shocked at the poor physical condition of the POWs. Until proper food supplies could arrive, they distributed boxes of their personal rations, which the POWs devoured.

In addition to being Good Friday, March 30 was also the second day of Passover.

Paul Stern reminded Skip Friedman of the vow they'd made that they'd survive this ordeal and be celebrating the Passover holiday in freedom.

Skip recalled that when an American tank pulled up to the gate of the camp, Lester, Paul, and I went out to greet it. An American soldier stuck his head out and yelled, "Anybody here from Ohio?"

"Me!" Skip shouted back.

"You have any food?" Paul asked.

The soldier pulled out some hard crackers and threw them over. Paul looked at the crackers, slapped them with his hands, and said, "I told you we'd have matzoh for Passover."

25
AT LAST!

"My stomach is full again and I'm too happy to say any more," Frankie wrote in his journal after the camp was liberated by the American forces. "I have an awful lot to talk about when I return to Lucy."

The American troops didn't have an evacuation plan for the POWs. They were no longer prisoners, but they had to wait a week to leave. During that time, the American POWs experienced role reversal: the American forces captured large numbers of retreating German troops and brought them into the camp, where the former POWs had the chance to act as the guards. This time it was the Germans who were forced into formations and held as prisoners of war.

When the American soldiers asked for volunteers to guard the Germans, Sonny jumped at the chance. He didn't want revenge; he wanted the better food rations that were offered as pay.

Sonny took up his position in the guard tower. He admitted that he didn't make a very good guard. He often fell asleep at his post.

Even before the US Army chow trucks arrived, the GIs discovered that the Germans had hidden huge amounts of potatoes in some straw. The men ate their first solid food since they were captured. Unfortunately, their digestive systems could barely tolerate even the bland boiled potatoes. Almost every one of the POWs was overcome with diarrhea, headaches, and disorientation. Solid food was too much for their stomachs. Some of the men could barely walk or stand up. Some had dropped from 170 pounds to 90 pounds.

Rather than wait for food to arrive, Skip Friedman and Paul Stern decided to go find food on their own. This was a risky decision considering their emaciated and weakened condition. Skip, Paul, and two others left on a mission to get some better food, clothing, cigarettes, and medicine. They had learned that there was an army depot near Frankfurt, about ninety miles away. They borrowed a truck and barreled down the highway without stopping. They came back with food, rations, candy, clothing, cough medicine, and other supplies. They were pleased that they had the strength and stamina to make the journey.

After eating, most of the former POWs suffered from the "trots"—diarrhea. Some cases were quite severe, even life-threatening. The medics like Paul knew that some of these cases could quickly cause death. Several large trucks were sent to carry out the men who were in the worst shape. On Easter Sunday, some of the most severely ill were taken to an airfield to be transported to a hospital on the west coast of France.

The men who were left waiting in the camp—including Roddie, Frankie, Lester, Paul, and Skip—tried to find moments of humor in their grim situation. Lester, at six feet, had dropped from 180 pounds to 120. He realized that he now weighed about the same as one of his petite girlfriends back home. When the men stripped off their shirts to shower, they couldn't hide the shock at their own skeletal physiques. Someone joked they looked like walking xylophones or piano keyboards. "You could have played any kind of music you like on our ribs," said one POW.

Once the idea of freedom sank in, the soldiers had time to think about what they had been through. Lester still marveled at Roddie's selflessness and courage standing up to Major Siegmann and refusing under the threat of death to obey the orders to evacuate the camp for the final death march.

"We weren't *liberated*," Lester said. "We escaped." Years later, Lester would say he was part of one of the "greatest mass escapes in World War II"—nearly 1,300 infantrymen liberating themselves from Nazi captivity.

Roddie didn't need credit or honors. He just wanted

to enjoy the peace. He didn't talk much about his feelings now that he was a free man, not even to his closest buddies, Frankie and Lester. Instead, he wrote in his journal. "I have made new friends and lost some," Roddie wrote. "I don't know whether all of my boys are alive or not. But I pray that they are. It all seems sort of a bad dream—a *very* bad one."

Seven days after the American troops liberated the camp, a long convoy of trucks arrived. The men cheered. "To an infantryman, trucks not only promise an end to the day's march, but a journey to somewhere better," wrote one former POW. "Trucks were the magic carpet to somewhere, anywhere else."

It took several more days, until April 10, 1945, for the former prisoners to be taken away from the camp. They drove down desolate German roads, past German towns and villages marked with white flags of surrender fluttering from open windows. Roddie, Frankie, and Lester rode side by side, uncomfortably cold in the open trucks. Frankie pointed out that all of the German towns and villages had been destroyed. Many were little more than piles of debris.

He remarked to Roddie and Lester that he was astonished by the Nazi determination to continue in this losing cause. "With all the food supplies that the US Army uncovered, it's pretty clear that Germany wanted to fight to the bitter end," he said.

After hours of traveling in the rattling uncovered trucks, they reached what was left of a Nazi airport where many army transport planes were waiting. For many of the men, this would be their first flight. It took a little more than two and a half hours in a heavy prop plane to reach France. When they arrived, they piled back into trucks and were driven to a camp for Returning Army Military Personnel, which they soon learned was called a RAMP camp. It was a tent city, with thousands of tents set up in rows.

"Out of Germany at last!" Frankie wrote in his journal on the day they arrived at the camp.

Roddie and many of his men were assigned to the RAMP called Lucky Strike, named for the cigarette brand. The other camps were named Camp Chesterfield, Camp Philip Morris, and Camp Old Gold. The men appreciated the names because many of them were smokers and tobacco had been a precious commodity in the camps, but the real reason for the cigarette names was security. By referring to the camps by names rather than locations, any Nazis listening in to Allied radio signals would think they were talking about cigarettes.

At Camp Lucky Strike, all the former POWs were registered and debriefed. A field hospital staffed with doctors and nurses checked all the men for lice, malnutrition, respiratory ailments, and untreated wounds of any kind. They issued the soldiers new clothing, and their filthy old uniforms—the same clothes the men had been wearing since the fall of 1944—were burned.

The men were also given vitamins, milk, and food. "A glass of grapefruit juice almost killed me," Paul Stern said. Overeating was a serious health concern in the early days at Camp Lucky Strike. "Some kids got terribly sick because their stomachs had shrunk," Paul said. "In fact, one fellow at Lucky Strike gorged himself and he didn't make it."

When they first reached Lucky Strike, the Red Cross offered the men doughnuts and coffee. The men ate too much and it shocked their digestive systems. "One unfortunate put away eighteen doughnuts and promptly died," Paul said. "In the next days, we were switched to eggnog and other more appropriate food."

Though Roddie, Lester, Skip, Paul, and Sonny gradually gained weight and regained their strength, other men from their group had to be taken to the hospital for additional care. Hank Freedman—who weighed less than 110 pounds at five feet, five inches—needed to spend four weeks in the hospital to manage his malnutrition.

Roddie and his group of nearly 1,300 men were the first American POWs to arrive back in Allied control. They didn't think of themselves as heroes, but they were given a hero's welcome. Lester was grateful for the respect they received from the people they encountered. "We were cleaned up, given new clothes, fed well and plenty, and treated like babies," Lester said. "We all got promotions, we were given awards. I got three battle stars and ribbons and I was putting on weight very rapidly." The stay at Camp Lucky Strike was brief—only four days—but few of the soldiers would ever forget it.

The mood changed on April 12, when news came over the radio announcing President Franklin Delano Roosevelt had died unexpectedly in Warm Springs, Georgia, at the age of sixty-three. The soldiers stood in silence, listening to the news, some wiping tears from their eyes.

"Although I was born while Calvin Coolidge was president, and lived through the disaster of Herbert Hoover, my first awareness of matters political started with FDR," Sonny said. "In all those years of growing up, going to school, and fighting a war, he was the only president I had known."

Lester was devastated. "FDR was our hero," he said. "We didn't know what kind of president Truman would make. It was such a sad time."

Two days later, on April 14, 1945, the men piled into trucks again and drove sixty miles back to the place they'd first come ashore: Le Havre harbor. This time they wouldn't be forced to wade through the frigid North Atlantic surf while carrying backpacks loaded with equipment. Instead, they walked down a ramp to board the USS *General W. P. Richardson*, a 622-foot troop transport ship.

The *General Richardson* had only been in service since

October 1944. Frankie called it "the most beautiful ship" he'd ever seen. "It was spotlessly clean. Everything was pure white."

The liberated POWs were sent below deck where they discovered air-conditioned, spacious compartments—all spotlessly clean. The men marveled at the beautiful rooms. "The washroom was the best I'd seen since I left Camp Atterbury," Frankie wrote. "Clean porcelain wash basins, showers, crystal-clear mirrors, showers, real commodes, and best of all, hot and cold running water."

Frankie, Roddie, and Lester delighted in swapping stories of home, laughing as they enjoyed the simple pleasures of freedom again—shaving with sharp, double-edged razor blades, using proper shaving brushes to lather up their faces, and running water so hot it probably scalded their fingers.

While they were still anchored off the coast of France, they lined up for a dinner fit for a king: boiled ham, baked potatoes, cabbage and carrot stew, and bread with fresh butter. The fluffy white bread—so often taken for granted at home—now tasted like a delicacy. The soldiers grabbed four or five slices at a time, clearly trying to erase the memory of the black sawdust bread that had kept them alive for months. They also slurped down steaming cups of hot coffee, sweetened and lightened with cream, trying to forget the tasteless brown liquid that the Nazis had tried to pass off as coffee. "Boy, under conditions like this, it won't be long before I forget all I've been through, and it won't be long before I'll be good and fat," Frankie said.

At about 10:30 p.m., they pulled out of port. Before heading to the United States, the *General Richardson* was going to England to pick up some wounded soldiers and then join a convoy of other naval ships.

Almost immediately, they ran into trouble. German submarines had been spotted the night before in the English Channel.

The GIs watched as the crew prepared "ash cans"—navy slang for depth charges or underwater bombs—which launched, apparently hitting some German U-boats.

"Trouble seems to follow me every place I go, and I still have a whole ocean to cross yet," Frankie wrote in his journal while sitting in his cabin. "But I'm sure we'll make it alright. God is watching. . . . I won't feel really safe or happy again until I'm deep in Lucy's arms once more."

German U-boats weren't the only threat. The Nazis had thoroughly mined the English Channel, so the crew stopped to blast away at the mines still floating in the water.

Roddie, Frankie, and Lester awakened on Sunday morning, April 15, 1945, to a familiar bugle call reminding them of life on a "proper" military base, like Fort Jackson or Camp Atterbury, rather than a miserable prison like Stalag IXA. They washed with hot water, shaved, brushed their teeth, put on clean uniforms, and sat down to a huge breakfast. Frankie lit a pipe up on the deck and took in the sight of the springtime coast of England. He said the rosary that morning, alone, in the absence of a priest.

That afternoon, a memorial was held in honor of FDR. Later, on the deck of the ship, they followed the news of the services taking place back in the States, listening to the account of a special train taking the president to Washington from Georgia, and the military procession from Union Station to the White House with a crowd of five hundred thousand people watching silently in the April sun. After a simple funeral service, FDR's coffin was taken back to Union Station, then placed aboard a train to be taken for burial at his home in Hyde Park, New York. Lester, Roddie, and Frankie stood in respectful silence, saluting when the flag on the *General Richardson* was lowered to half-mast. The flag would remain lowered for the rest of the journey home.

On April 16, the *General Richardson* pulled into the port of Southampton. A new group of soldiers were brought on board—men who had lost legs, arms, and eyes. Some men suffered from severe shell shock—what we now call post-traumatic stress—and they were muttering to themselves, flinching, quivering, talking excitedly to shadows. "It made me feel lucky," Frankie wrote in his journal.

Once the men were on board, the *General Richardson* joined

a twelve-ship convoy, and at 6:00 p.m., the men started for home. Most of the men were too relieved to be free to worry about how dangerous the Atlantic passage was.

The Nazis should not have been a problem any longer. By the time they were heading back to the United States, the Germans had all but lost the war. Roddie, Frankie, and Lester had learned from the radio that day, American troops had reached the city of Nuremberg, the spiritual heart of the Third Reich and the stage for massive Nazi Party rallies. Many of Hitler's speeches and announcements had been made there. From his bombproof bunker in Berlin, Hitler had ordered his troops to protect the city at all costs. When some German soldiers waved white flags and tried to surrender to Americans, they were mowed down by machine-gun fire from their fellow Nazis. There weren't enough German troops to defend the cities. The Nazis armed children as young as fifteen with rifles and grenades and ordered them to fight. There was no hope of German victory.

But that didn't mean that they were out of danger. Even in those final weeks of the war, the Nazi U-boats remained extremely active. Frankie told Roddie that he was afraid they'd come all this way—survived the Battle of the Bulge, the horror of the Christmastime railyard bombing, and the hell of the camps—only to be sunk by a torpedo of some U-boat captain too headstrong, or maybe too clueless, to realize that the Nazi cause was lost.

There was nothing they could do to change the situation, so the men tried not to think about any possible risks. Instead, they spent time with their friends, playing cards and rolling dice.

The soldiers found a record player on board. They could find only one record, the Andrews Sisters' "Rum and Coca-Cola," a hit from 1945. They played the song over and over again. Many men laid out in the sun, tanning their faces and chests.

For the next few days, the weather changed: the seas were rough and the air was cold and misty. One day when the seas were particularly choppy, Frankie wrote in his journal, "It's a darn good thing I'm not allergic to seasickness."

The weather then changed again, and by April 20 the temperature was so hot and the sun so strong that the men wished they had sunglasses and bathing trunks. They also celebrated when they heard that the German city of Nuremberg had fallen at last. "A great birthday present for Adolf," said one of the soldiers, noting that it was Adolf Hitler's fifty-sixth birthday.

The reason for the change in weather was that in order to avoid U-boat activity, the captain had plotted a course far to the south. It meant more days at sea, but a safer route. "I don't mind going home the hard way, as long as it's the *safe* way," Frankie told Roddie and Lester. That night in his journal Frankie wrote: "Another day gone by, and another pound of fat gained. I actually look human now."

In the days that followed, the men began to feel more anxious. April 23 was Frankie's birthday, but he remained in a sour mood. "This makes three years that I haven't had a birthday at home," he wrote in his journal. "That sure makes me mad. Just another day gone by. Gosh, but these days seem long and endless. Seems like we'll never reach home."

No matter how they tried to distract themselves, the closer they got to home, the more the men began to feel a strange and unexpected sense of panic. Soldiers who had held tight to memories of home during the Battle of the Bulge and the months in the camps now worried that their loved ones and the world they'd left behind had moved on without them; there might not be a place for them.

Roddie worried about trying to reconnect with his ex-wife, Marie. What if she wouldn't agree to reconcile? Who was he going home to?

On April 25, 1945, Frankie wrote in his journal: "I'm half-afraid to go home and I'm sick with worry. I keep thinking what if things have changed? What if there's trouble at home? What if something has happened? Will Lucy be the same or has she changed? That worries me more than anything. God. I wish I were home now."

The next day Frankie told Roddie that he couldn't sleep. "I didn't sleep a wink all night long," Frankie said. "Just can't seem to get Lucy and home off my mind. Well, anyway we dock Saturday and leave the ship at eight o'clock. Saturday, please hurry up. It's just anxiety that's got me—nothing else."

Finally, after they'd been crossing the Atlantic for two weeks, the New York coastline came into view. White and red lights flickered through the predawn darkness and sea mist. In the morning, swarms of small vessels loaded with civilians came out to greet the returning soldiers. When the *General Richardson* sailed into New York Harbor on April 28, the men crowded the deck, straining to get a glimpse of Brooklyn and Manhattan. When the Statue of Liberty came into view, her distinctive green-bronze figure bathed in sunlight, the soldiers cheered. "We figured that we had helped keep her safe too," said one of the soldiers.

From the docks of Brooklyn, the soldiers were taken to Camp Kilmer at New Brunswick, New Jersey, for another round of processing and debriefing. Roddie and the men liberated from Stalag IXA were one of the first large groups of returning US troops.

"We were almost treated like celebrities," Lester later said. He was one of the ex-POWs who'd been asked to participate in a radio interview. "I called my parents: 'Tune into this New Jersey station—I'm going to be interviewed.' After I was captured, they'd informed my family that I was missing in action and they didn't know if I was alive or dead until the month before I was liberated. The news didn't travel very quickly, so they were just overjoyed to hear my voice."

All the men were issued passes for sixty-two-day furloughs—a virtually unheard-of amount of time, but an appreciation of the hard months they'd spent in Nazi captivity. The men had their teeth checked and cleaned. Afterward, Lester invited Paul home with him. "Paul, our apartment is just a few blocks further down. You want to come over and meet my mother?"

"Sure," Paul said. "Why not?"

In their crisply pressed uniforms, nodding at passersby, they walked down to 170th Street. When they got out of the elevator and entered the apartment, they saw that Lester's mother had prepared a huge spread of food—corned beef and pastrami, fresh rye bread, kosher dill pickles, a dish of kasha varnishkes, fresh melon and berries, honey cake, éclairs, and bottles of milk. A feast like that would help them gain back some of the fifty to eighty pounds they'd lost during their ordeal.

"We sat there gorging ourselves on these delicious éclairs," Paul recalled. "After about ten minutes, the French doors to the dining room opened and Lester's sister, Corinne, appeared. When I saw her, I fell in love. And I said to myself, 'That's the girl I'm going to marry.' At that very moment. And that's what happened. That was the moment I fell in love with her. And we were married two years later."

* * *

Hitler committed suicide in his bunker on April 30. The war with Germany was over, but the fighting continued in the Pacific. Roddie, Lester, Frankie, Paul, Skip, Hank, and Sonny realized that their service wasn't over. They could all end up back in combat, very soon, only this time fighting against the Japanese.

Lester and Sonny went to Lake Placid for two weeks of R & R, rest and relaxation. Lester was promoted to staff sergeant and then assigned back to Fort Benning, Georgia. He was training for an invasion of Japan. "The war was still raging in the Pacific," Lester said. "It was pretty hot. We were battling on Iwo Jima, island-hopping, but everyone knew that in order to defeat Japan, we would have to invade the main island. MacArthur was getting together as many troops as possible to eventually make that invasion. I was part of that division."

Lester didn't know about the Manhattan Project, a top secret mission the United States was running to develop the atomic bomb. He was preparing to go overseas in August 1945, when he learned about the US bombing of Hiroshima on August 5. Two days later, the United States dropped a second bomb on Nagasaki. The Japanese surrendered.

"I was saved by President Truman deciding to drop those atomic bombs," Lester said. "He was widely criticized. I *never* criticized him. He probably saved a million lives, including mine. First Roddie. Then President Truman. I knew I was going to survive, come back, start my life."

On August 8, 1945, it seemed like the war was finally over. Life could start again. "I'd served my country," said Lester, who was twenty-two years old at the time. "We were victorious. The Japanese were defeated. The Nazis were defeated. And life was beautiful."

Roddie didn't speak about the early days when he returned to the United States. While he was still in Germany, he wrote about a life of love, friendship, and faith that he planned to lead from that day forward. "I am going back home to my relatives and friends," Roddie wrote. "I feel as if I am going to be strange among them. I want no sympathy, I want peace, quiet, and more than anything I want God. I hope my actions won't cause the wrong feeling towards me. I don't want to do anything wrong, not the least little thing."

In the pages of the journal, he considered that his family and friends would never be able to understand his wartime experiences. He found it impossible to express his precise feelings about everything he'd been through in the past six months.

"There is a lot more I would like to say, but I don't know how," Roddie wrote in the final entry of his journal. "I have kind of poured my heart out here, and it is foolish I guess, but as I said at the beginning, I wanted to get it off my chest. I don't think I would ever have nerve enough to tell anyone this, but I feel as if I can let it be read. I would like to repeat, I have only been overseas a little less than six months, but I have got a good idea what combat is. You've got to be there to know."

PART THREE

THE STORY LIVES ON

26
BE THE HERO

I didn't know my father's story until after he died. I had always loved him and knew he had loved me, but only after I learned about his combat experience did I feel that I really *knew* him.

The father I had known growing up had been full of life and a sincere person of faith. But like most dads I knew, he had been so ordinary—even flawed. Yet my transformative journey had revealed something greater. While Dad's life had been marked by tragedy and hardships, it had been well lived and deeply felt. I know that now. My father wasn't perfect; none of ours are. But what I've learned is that you don't have to be perfect to do something extraordinary. Ordinary people are heroic, and an ordinary life lived well is, indeed, extraordinary. My father's story is a testament to that. And so are the stories of the men who served alongside him, the men my father saved in Stalag IXA. Like ripples in a pond,

my father's actions all those years ago continue to reso-
nate today, in unexpected ways. In doing this research on
my father's past, I found that my father had lots of experiences I knew nothing about. I knew that he had fought in
both World War II and the Korean War before meeting my
mom, but the details of his earlier years had been largely
unknown to me and my older brother, Mike. In early January 2016, while doing research about my father's wartime
experiences, I asked my mom what she knew about Dad's
past. How much did she know about my father before his
enlistment in the military?

She casually mentioned that my father had been married before he met her. She said that Dad had married his
high school sweetheart, Marie, before going into the army.
Then he had received a letter from Marie breaking up with
him, followed by divorce papers, just before shipping out
to Europe. After his World War II service, he returned to
Knoxville to try to fix their relationship, but things didn't
work out.

After my mom told me about Marie, she added—as if it
was common knowledge—that I had a sister from Dad's first
marriage. I had no idea that I had a half sister, although she
apparently knew about me. I learned that she had lived in
Knoxville all her life, although we had never met. It's quite
possible that I had crossed paths with her during my college
days, when I sometimes bought hot dogs at Paul's Market, a

store owned by her husband, Paul.

In January 2016, I met my sister, Priscilla Edmonds Davenport, and Paul, for the first time. I immediately knew she was my sister. She was a petite, attractive, well-dressed, energetic lady—a devout Christian who had the unmistakable "look" of an Edmonds. Although she was twelve years older, we bonded instantly. We're still close today.

Priscilla was born in Knoxville on January 30, 1945, just three days after our dad stood up to the commander on behalf of the Jewish men in his unit. My father didn't get to spend much time with his daughter. He visited her after World War II, but Marie's father didn't like Roddie and forbade him to see Marie and Priscilla. Later, Marie remarried and stayed in the same South Knoxville neighborhood where she and Roddie had met.

By connecting with Priscilla, I began the process of healing what had been one of the most painful moments in my father's life. His divorce from Marie devastated him; he felt cut off from what he thought was going to be his future. "I had lost what I had wanted all my life, a home, a wife, and happiness," he wrote in the POW camp. Because of my Christian faith—the faith I learned from my father—I'm quite certain he would be pleased to know that his daughter, Priscilla, and I have connected. Ultimately, Dad's brave actions in Stalag IXA not only saved his men but have led to repairing a breach in the family that he so desperately wanted more than seventy years ago.

I'm not sure why Dad never told me or my brother about Marie or Priscilla. Perhaps, like his POW experiences, they were locked away in his vault of wartime memories, never to be seen or heard of again. Maybe those memories were simply too painful. Most likely it was because my father—like all the GIs I've met—enjoyed the days he was living and looked forward in hope to tomorrow. For me, meeting and getting to know my sister has been one of the many blessings of learning more about my father's life.

Another great blessing has been meeting some of the men who served with my father and survived the POW camps during World War II. I love these men and their families. Along with Dad, they are heroes and great examples for us. They served our country well during World War II and overcame the same hellish POW camps as Dad. Somehow their experiences during the war didn't defeat them but rather inspired them to return to the United States, finish college, marry their sweethearts, raise families, and lead ordinary lives of extraordinary influence.

My dad's legacy lies in these men and their children, grandchildren, great-grandchildren, and the generations to come. One day while I was sitting in the solitude of the Library of Congress, I began to calculate the full impact of my father's bravery. Lester and Skip estimated that about two hundred Jewish men were saved when my father ordered his men to claim that the soldiers were all Jews. And nearly thirteen hundred soldiers were saved two months later when dad and his men refused to leave the camp. Most of these men then had children, grandchildren, and great-grandchildren. We estimated that due to Dad's courageous actions in the POW camp, it is likely that more than *twelve thousand* people are alive today.

As part of my research, I wanted to meet as many of the men who served with my father as I could find. I am still on that journey.

In 2014, I drove down to meet with Hank Freedman, who lived about thirty-five miles north of Atlanta. Hank was ninety years old, living in a one-bedroom apartment near his loving family. He was suntanned, had a full head of white hair, and he sat straight and strong in his armchair.

Hank told me that the grandmother who raised him fainted when he telephoned her from New York City on May 8, 1945. She wasn't sure she'd ever see him again. After the war, Hank enjoyed a successful business career, making frequent trips to East Asia as a buyer for Rich's department store in Atlanta. He survived cancer and was married for fifty-one years before his lovely wife, Betty, died in 2004. The walls of the study in Hank's home—his "prayer closet," where he studied the scriptures and prayed daily—were decorated with his World War II medals and badges, as well as other awards and memorabilia of his family and career.

Hank said that Roddie's demonstration of faith in the boxcar had influenced the rest of his life. "It had an effect on me," Hank said. "Here it is more than seventy years later, and I remember that incident very vividly. Roddie's faith amazed me. It was my first seed of faith."

Hank's decision to become a born-again Christian was just one of the extraordinary acts of faith I discovered while on my journey.

Another remarkable act of faith was one I heard about from Paul and Corinne Stern, and from their daughter, Joanne, during my first visit to their home in Reston, Virginia, just outside Washington, DC. Paul kept his World War II memorabilia in his den. One of the items he treasured was a fragile piece of yellowed paper, the official notification sent to Paul's mother that her son was missing in action, followed by a notice that he was being held as a prisoner of war.

When she read the telegram, Paul's mother vowed to observe the Sabbath from that moment on. She would observe God's day of rest and do no work—she would not even turn on a light switch—from sundown on Friday until sunset on Saturday. She promised God that if her son survived, she would "remember the Sabbath day, to keep it holy," for the rest of her life.

Paul's daughter, Joanne, told me the impact her

grandmother's decision had on her as a twelve-year-old girl. "There isn't a week that goes by that I don't think about my grandmother's commitment," Joanne said. "She made a commitment to observe the Sabbath, which included not driving in a car or even carrying an umbrella. I remember the night of my bat mitzvah, a Friday evening, we were all going to the synagogue and it was raining cats and dogs." Corinne and her family drove to the Temple Sholom a couple of miles from their home, but her grandmother insisted on walking. Paul walked with her.

"They kept walking in that downpour, in the pitch-dark, all the way to the synagogue," Joanne said. "Every few blocks my mom would stop the car and my grandmother would get in. We had towels and we would dry her off." She would rest for a minute and then go back out in the rain. "She went right back out and continued to walk to the synagogue with my father by her side. I vividly remember the beautiful blue silk suit that she wore."

"Chris, I think we've lost the definition of commitment and discipline."

I agreed. "I deeply admire a mom, having her son lost in action overseas, crying out to God, making a vow and then living that commitment."

"And what's important is teaching it to children," Joanne said. "I've shared this story with my own children over and over again, as an example of the kind of commitment and discipline my grandmother had."

Her son Paul also had that kind of commitment and discipline.

On March 30, 2017, at age ninety-three, Paul passed away in Virginia, surrounded by his loving family. It was seventy-two years to the day after his liberation from Stalag IXA. Paul's last message to his children and grandchildren was about love: with pen and paper, he drew a heart to illustrate his desire for them to remain close, asking them to make his treasured retreat in East Hampton, Long Island, a place to love and share with one another.

Like Hank and Paul, Skip Friedman became another friend. Skip devoted his life to issues involving social justice, a choice that may have stemmed from his POW experiences. Even in his nineties, Skip was vibrant and full of life. In addition to having been a star football player, an avid historian, and an accomplished lawyer, he could also act and sing. After the war Skip sang in a barbershop quartet and appeared as a spear carrier in the opera *Aida*.

Like my father, Skip possessed profound moral clarity and was a man utterly without prejudice. When Skip's daughter was a senior in high school, she became best friends with a student visiting from West Germany. The girl actually lived with Skip's family for a year and they learned that her father had been a German soldier in World War II. He did not judge the girl based on the actions of her father.

In their retirement years, Skip and his wife, Penny, traveled the world, enjoyed tennis and music, and volunteered with their local reform synagogue and numerous political groups. Skip served on the board of directors of several hospitals in Ohio. He cared for Penny through her battle with dementia until she died, after more than sixty-five years of marriage.

As a widower, Skip continued living with astonishing zeal: still practicing law and enjoying the company of his ten grandchildren. He cherished each day and touched countless others with his brilliant mind, optimism, and generosity. Cared for by medical staff of the Cleveland VA hospital, Skip died peacefully on February 23, 2017, in his Shaker Heights home, at age ninety-two, surrounded by his loved ones, stacks of his books, and photos of his beloved Penny.

I never met Frankie Cerenzia, but I did meet his daughter, Lorna Nocero, in 2018. I had searched online for records of the men in my dad's journal and found that a "Frank Cerenzia, Staff-Sergeant, World War II" is buried in a veterans cemetery in East Farmingdale, Suffolk County, New York. Luckily, "Cerenzia" is not a common surname, and through some ancestry detective work, I found records of Frank and Lucille, and the married names of their daughters. With that information, I made a cold call to a high school in New York where I thought Frankie's daughter worked. It turned out I was right—I'd hit the bull's-eye: Lorna was indeed Frankie's daughter.

When my wife and I met Lorna, she had brought a folder of letters, pictures, news clippings, and a copy of the journal that her dad had kept in the POW camps. His notebook looked exactly like the one my father had used.

"Where did they get the books?" my wife, Regina, asked.

"The International Red Cross was giving them out," I said, carefully cracking open the notebook, each page filled with Frankie's seventy-five-year-old script, each day of his captivity meticulously dated. The words were so clear, it seemed as if they'd been written yesterday.

"Your father's got great handwriting," I said. I glanced down at a random page and the words jumped out at me. "On the 18th of January the Germans showed their true colors. They segregated all the Jews from the gentiles." I knew the story.

"'Roddie Edmonds was also one of us,'" I read aloud from Frank's journal. "'Roddie and I have been together so far since the very beginning of my army career up until now. We will continue to be very close to each other even after we've been discharged and sent home. He lives in Knoxville, Tennessee.'"

Of all the men who served with Dad during the war,

Frankie's life was the shortest. Lorna explained that her dad—a lifelong cigarette smoker—developed heart disease while in his forties. At the time, there was little Frankie's doctors could do. He suffered a massive heart attack and died at age forty-nine in October 1973. Lorna was just twenty-two. "I feel like he died before my life even began," she said.

Frankie returned to Brooklyn after his discharge from the army. He and Lucy lived in the Marine Park section of the borough. He became a hardworking Italian American father. He made enough money selling insurance that he was able to build a nice home in Howard Beach, Queens, in 1966. Frankie died seven years after moving into his dream house; Lorna still lives in it with her husband and children.

Like Roddie, Frankie had never talked to his family about his wartime experiences. I asked Lorna if she had ever noticed any sign that he had gone through trauma during the war.

"My father was the jolliest man," she said. "He never seemed like he was in a bad mood. My mother would be grumpy, but my father was always chipper—always positive. If you came to him with a problem, he always had a positive attitude."

It was another common thread I'd noticed, with my dad, Lester, Skip, Paul, and so many of the other guys: never take tomorrow for granted; always live in the present.

"Lorna," I said, "your dad reminds me of Skip Friedman. He told me, 'Chris, since I left that POW camp, I've *never* had a bad day. Not one—ever.'"

"I'm sure they just appreciated being alive," Lorna said.

"Actually, Skip told me: 'We *died* in that camp—and we were reborn.'"

A famous passage in the Talmud—the source of Jewish religious law and theology—reads: "Anyone who saves a single life, it is as if he saved an entire world."

I believe that with all my heart. That's why I am spreading Dad's message, telling the world about the transformative power of selfless sacrifice and moral courage—sacrifice and moral courage anyone can give.

In the library of the Harvard Club, Lester had asked me, "Chris, do you know your congressman in Tennessee? You should tell the story to him and see if he agrees about the Medal of Honor. If he does, then you should seek his help."

As I drove back home with Regina and Austin, I realized that my life had taken a new direction, a new mission: I had the opportunity—indeed, the obligation—to inspire people everywhere with Dad's story.

In Tennessee, my congressman, Jimmy Duncan, heard the account of my father's heroism and agreed that Roddie Edmonds deserved the Medal of Honor. He asked Tennessee senators Lamar Alexander and Bob Corker to join the effort. An entire team of Tennesseans went to work gathering death certificates of superior officers, historical information regarding the camp, actions taken, eyewitness testimony—all to help recognize what my dad did.

While I traveled around the country to meet the men Dad saved, Lester remained actively involved in the Medal of Honor efforts. He often said that the "defining moment of his life"—from the military through Harvard Law School and beyond—stemmed from Roddie's actions on that bitter-cold January morning in Stalag IXA.

"The lesson of that day has shaped my life," Lester wrote in an affidavit for the Medal of Honor recommendation. "There have been times when you must take a calculated risk, however perilous, to stand up and do the right thing for yourself and those for whom you have responsibility. Roddie's courage influenced me to attend law school with the help of the GI Bill. One man's courage saved many lives, mine among them. When I look back at all the years since that fateful day, I find many occasions in my personal, family, and professional life when I can link my decisions and actions to my service in the war and to that experience when I watched Roddie standing up to the Nazi major. I am still doing that now—at age ninety."

On June 6, 2015—the seventy-first anniversary of D-Day—I received an unexpected phone call from the Consulate General of Israel in Atlanta, relaying the news that Yad Vashem, Israel's national Holocaust memorial, had decided to honor my father for extraordinary bravery in saving Jewish GIs during World War II. Thanks to the tireless efforts of my dear friends Larry and Barbara Goldstein, the consulate informed me that my dad, Master Sergeant Roddie Edmonds of Knoxville, Tennessee, would be honored in Jerusalem as one of the Righteous Among the Nations, the highest honor a Gentile can receive from the State of Israel.

Only four other Americans have received this honor: Vivian Fry, Lois Gunden, and Martha and Waitstill Sharp. No other US serviceman ever has. Our family is forever grateful.

In mid-December 2015, I made my first visit to Israel. I'd gone to Jerusalem not only to honor Dad, but to study the Holocaust with Christian leaders.

Standing at the gates of Yad Vashem, the World Holocaust Remembrance Center, I began reading Isaiah 56:5, etched above their entrance: "And to them will I give in my house and within my walls a memorial and a name that shall not be cut off."

I could scarcely believe I was there. Transfixed by the passage of scripture, I thought about the events more than seventy years before, when a Nazi major held a pistol to my father's head and said, "Sergeant . . . you will order the Jews to step forward or I will shoot you right now."

I do not know how my father survived. No one expected the Nazis to give in.

But the Nazis *did* give in.

I thought about the final days of the war, when the American POWs were ordered to line up outside the barracks to march out, and my father convinced his men to defy the order. He knew his men would die if they left the camp.

I do not know how my father survived.

But the Nazis *did* give in. Again.

Reading Isaiah 56 again, I brushed a tear from my cheek. *I'm alive. I'm more alive than I've ever been.*

As I ran to catch up to my group, I thanked God for saving Dad and his men and for giving my father the moral courage to be as "bold as a lion."

"A 'Righteous' is a non-Jew who helps Jews, someone who decided to leave the position of the bystander, someone willing to pay a price," said Irena Steinfeldt, Yad Vashem's director of the Department for the Righteous Among the Nations. "Someone who risked himself in order to help a Jew . . . someone who was willing to share the fate of the Jews." Irena explained: "It's an attempt to recognize that every person is responsible for their deeds. Every person has a choice between good and evil."

There are some twenty-seven thousand Righteous Gentiles honored at Yad Vashem, but my father's case is unique. "It was the first time we received a request to honor an

American for saving American Jews," Irena said. My father did not have to risk his life to save his fellow POWs. "He didn't have to do that," she said. "He could have said, *I have paid my dues. I have done everything for my country. I'm a patriot. I served my country well.* He went the extra mile. It's a story that shows you in whatever situation, wherever you are, no matter how bad it can be, a person can always make a difference."

All of this attention would almost certainly confuse and embarrass Dad, who thought he was just doing what he had to do. If he were alive today, he would probably ask, "Son, what's all the fuss? I opposed the enemy, I protected my men, I honored God. I was just doing my job."

In fact, that's what President Barack Obama said on International Holocaust Remembrance Day in 2016. President Obama was speaking at the Righteous Among the Nations Award Ceremony, introduced by filmmaker Steven Spielberg.

"I know your dad said he was just doing his job, Chris, but he went above and beyond the call of duty," President Obama said. "Faced with a choice of giving up his fellow soldiers or saving his own life, Roddie looked evil in the eye and dared a Nazi to shoot. His moral compass never wavered. He was true to his faith, and he saved some two hundred Jewish American soldiers as a consequence. It's an instructive lesson, by the way, for those of us Christians. I cannot imagine a greater expression of Christianity than to say, 'I too am a Jew.'"

Dad loved all his men. As Lester Tanner said at the Righteous ceremony, "Roddie could no more have turned over any of his men to the Nazis than he could stop breathing." To Dad, his actions weren't an act of valor; they were simply the right thing to do.

Faith—and his military training—had given Dad a deep sense of right and wrong. His moral clarity allowed him to focus and see evil for what it was, and the courage to stand firm, even with a pistol pressed to his forehead.

Under the harshest conditions, my father and the other POWs discovered that life is a precious gift. From their day of liberation forward, nothing was taken for granted: each breath of fresh air, each morsel of bread, each cup of coffee, was something my father and the other POWs appreciated.

My father's bravery was contagious. Any one of the men could have given in to fear and turned over the Jewish Americans in their ranks. But they didn't. They stood strong because they stood together.

I'm often asked why I think my father did what he did, why he stood resolute even when facing the threat of point-blank execution.

I asked Lester, and he said he thought it was my father's sense of duty as a soldier to do what was right for his men and fight back against the Germans in any way he could. It was my father's way of remaining a proud US infantryman and bringing honor to his country, even without his beloved M1 rifle.

I think it's because of Dad's faith. If he were by my side today, if I could ask him why he did what he did in Stalag IXA in January 1945, I'm nearly certain what his answer would be: my father was willing to die to save Jewish men under his command because he believed a Jewish man—Jesus Christ—had died to save him.

Dad's life flowed from one eternal truth he believed—that God is real and God is good. And Dad was convinced that God's love, though free, had one *essential* responsibility—we must be good to one another. To Dad it was simple. He loved God. He loved others. And love gave him the courage to do what was right for humanity even in the face of death.

Growing up, I had no idea that my dad had risked his life to save two hundred Jewish American servicemen. I had no idea that he risked his life again to save nearly 1,300 starving American POWs from leaving on a death march. As a kid in Knoxville, my dad was just the jovial guy with the booming baritone voice that everyone loved. He was the volunteer coach teaching my buddies and me how to hook slide into second base. He was simply "Dad," a regular guy chomping on one of his Dutch Masters "chewin' seegars" as he mowed our lawn on steamy Tennessee summer evenings.

Even then he was my hero.

I think what's most remarkable about my journey to discover what my father did in World War II is the realization that any *one* of us has the untapped potential to do something incredibly courageous. It could be the most unassuming person—a grandmother wheeling her cart through a supermarket or a teacher welcoming her students with a smile, a teenage boy hunched over a book at an airport gate, or a young soldier in harm's way—we all have the potential to change the world simply by standing up for what's right.

True heroes, I've learned, are rarely the larger-than-life characters of comic books or Hollywood blockbusters. They walk among us—like my dad did—virtually unnoticed, every day. They make the world a better place, quietly, anonymously—one person, one action, at a time.

AFTERWORD

The journey that began around a kitchen table with my daughter led me to other kitchen tables, into other living rooms of men who still held on to vivid recollections of what they went through all those years ago. And just like my dad, few had ever shared those experiences with their family. We shed lots of tears, shared many poignant moments in those homes. Over time, they became family.

And my fascinating journey continues. I hope it never ends. It's been a journey of life and love guided by the good Lord above. Without the small miracles of God's providence, and hundreds of helpful folks along the way, Dad's remarkable story—and the stories of the heroic men who served with him—would have remained lost and forgotten.

I'm blessed that Lester Tanner, a paragon of heroism, has become my friend and mentor. His practical wisdom and positive spirit make him a natural confidant. I'm certain my father saw the same qualities in him.

When I first met Lester, he was eighty-eight, full of energy, and still practicing law part-time. I found a man, who like my dad, loved life—he never took a single day for granted.

Lester has lived well. His indomitable spirit, positivity, and generosity have influenced me and many others. Like all the men I met who served with Dad, Lester has helped and inspired countless people in his legal career and everyday life, which has been the result of both hard work and ethical choices. Lester told me that what my father did back in Stalag IXA was a "life-changing experience. On that day in 1945, I made a promise to myself to *always* do the right thing," he said. "Particularly when you're an attorney and you must make moral decisions, you have to remind yourself to take the risk, to do the right thing."

At age ninety-five, Lester continues to keep that promise.

Sonny Fox, pioneering American television host, executive, and broadcasting consultant, has become yet another invaluable new friend. Regina and I first met Sonny—most famous for hosting the children's program *Wonderama* from 1959 to 1967—in New York. Once again, we were back in the Harvard Club, a guest of Lester's. It was September 2015. Sonny, still tall and lean, sported a white suit with a crisp burgundy striped oxford shirt, which accented his full head of silver hair. He brought me a copy of his memoir, *But*

You Made the Front Page! Wonderama, Wars, and a Whole Bunch of Life. Most of what I wanted to know about his time in World War II, he told me, was covered in his book. Sonny was the consummate entertainer, quick-witted, full of clever ad-libs and good-humored jabs. He reminisced about their time during the war, weaving in one-liners and anecdotes that had both Regina and me howling with laughter.

Later, we had the pleasure of sitting with Sonny and his beloved wife, Cely, in Los Angeles when Dad received a Medal of Valor from the Simon Wiesenthal Center along with the late Israeli prime minister Shimon Peres and Christian humanitarian Johnnie Moore. I'll always cherish my friendship with Sonny and Cely.

One deep regret I've felt is not having the opportunity to meet more of these heroic veterans—men like Jack Sherman and Ernest Kinoy. I was blessed to talk to Jack on the phone in September 2016, but before I could visit him in his hometown of Rochester, New York, he passed away in early 2017.

I'll never forget our conversation as Jack recalled my father's character. "Roddie was very tolerant of everybody," he said. "That's the kind of person he was. And you can rest assured that his religion did play a part in his personality. Chris, your father was loved by everybody. Sure, he was a tough sergeant, but he had a heart of gold."

Talking with Jack, hearing his stories about my father,

has been one of the highlights of my journey.

Ernest Kinoy is another remarkable World War II veteran and ex-POW who I wish I could have met. Ernie—as all his friends called him—went on to have an accomplished career as screenwriter, playwright, and president of the Writers Guild of America, East. Ernie had been locked in the same boxcar with Dad and Hank Freedman that terror-filled Christmas Eve of 1944. Somewhere along the journey, Ernie signed my dad's journal and, later, after being separated with the other Jewish privates at Bad Orb, miraculously survived both starvation and German brutality in the Berga slave-labor camp.

Reconnecting with my sister, Priscilla, has been an unexpected miracle. Just two weeks after our first meeting in Knoxville, Priscilla and her husband, Paul, joined us for the Righteous ceremony in Washington, DC. It helped her to see our father more clearly and contributed to her emotional healing. For me, it was a blessing to have her and Paul there. The desire Dad had expressed so long ago to heal his family and to have a relationship with his daughter was in the process of being fulfilled.

Recognized along with Dad posthumously at the Righteous ceremony in Washington were Lois Gunden of Goshen, Indiana, and Polish citizens Walery and Maryla Zbijewski of Warsaw. Gunden, a French teacher serving as a Mennonite missionary, established a children's home in southern France, where she sheltered Jews she'd helped smuggle out of a nearby internment camp. She even protected the children when French police showed up at the home. She was later detained by the Germans and released in a prisoner exchange. The Zbijewskis hid a Jewish child in their Warsaw home until the girl's mother could take her back. All are heroes who chose to risk their lives and love others in the face of unspeakable cruelty and evil.

"Too often, especially in times of change, especially in times of anxiety and uncertainty, we are too willing to give in to a base desire to find someone else, someone different, to blame for our struggles," President Obama said at the ceremony: "So here tonight we must confront the reality that around the world anti-Semitism is on the rise. We cannot deny it."

The Righteous ceremony was amazing. I hope that the next remarkable ceremony to honor Dad will happen if he is awarded the Medal of Honor or the Congressional Gold Medal.

I think all of us have been honored to know Dad's story and to have met just a few of the hundreds of thousands of noble men we call the "Greatest Generation." Those young men—many of them still boys just out of high school—marched into battle with a profound sense of patriotism and duty. All faced the unimaginable horrors of war. All fought with grit, honor, sacrifice, and dignity. They secured for us a world of freedom, a world free of the terrors of Nazism.

To this day, I remain in awe of them.

Since embarking on this journey, I've gone to places I never expected to visit, been introduced to people I never expected to meet, and learned truths about my father and humanity I never imagined. Each of us, I've come to understand, has the moral capacity to make a difference in the lives of others. Our everyday actions of goodwill are what help make our world a better place. What we often don't realize is that we're leaving a legacy every time we do something kind, generous, or thoughtful for someone else— simply because, as Lester said, it's "the right thing to do."

It's that simple.

I hope Dad's story inspires all of us to do what's right and look to the needs of others. As I often say, "When you wake up in the morning, think of others first and yourselves last."

The way I see it, many of our problems would be solved if we all lived that way.

ACKNOWLEDGMENTS

With profound gratitude, I acknowledge the following family and friends who helped me along the way. All of them are ordinary people making an extraordinary difference in our world.

To God: Thank you for everything. *All that we have accomplished you have done* (Isaiah 26:12).

To my dad, Roddie: Thank you for being my hero before I knew of your heroism. Earth and heaven are richer because of you.

To my mom, Mary Ann: Thank you for loving Dad and us well.

To my high school sweetheart and wife, Regina: Thank you for being my joy on my journey.

To my daughters and families: Alicia, Steve, Austin, Haylee, and Lilly; Kristen, Jed, Hagen, Holden, and Ruthie; Lauren, Ray, Maylee, Mollee, and Roderick. Thank you for loving God and inspiring our journey.

To my brother, Mike, who saved me from drowning when I was five: Keep fighting schizophrenia and helping Mom.

To my sister, Priscilla Davenport, and family: Meeting you has been one of my greatest joys. Thank you for sharing your unconditional love.

To Rodney Grubb and family: Thank you for your friendship since seventh grade and for cheering for Dad and his "boys."

To Rick Oster: Thank you for your friendship and for wanting to tell the story far and wide.

To Lester Tanner and family: Thank you for sharing Dad's story and inviting us to join your family's journey—a family we cherish.

To Paul and Corinne Stern and family: Thank you for enriching our lives with your family and love.

To Sydney "Skip" Friedman and family: Thank you for your love and making us feel like we are family.

To Irwin "Sonny" Fox and Cely: Thank you for showing us how to love deeply and have fun doing it.

To Henry "Hank" Freedman: Thank you for your friendship. You have been a highlight of my journey.

To Jack and Marcia Lou Sherman: Thank you for your wit and wisdom. I only wish we could have met.

To Lorna Nocero: Thank you for sharing stories about your wonderful dad and his love for others.

To Larry and Barbara Goldstein: Thank you for loving

us and for sharing Dad's story with Yad Vashem.

To my Yad Vashem friends: Thank you and the nation of Israel for honoring Dad so highly. Our family is forever grateful.

To Ambassador Ron Dermer and Yarden Golan: Thank you for your friendship and favor toward Dad.

To Erwin Stoff and Richard Abate: Thank you for loving Dad's story and believing in me.

To Douglas Century: Thank you for wanting to share Dad's story as much as I do and doing it so well.

To Winifred Conkling: Thank you for loving children and for helping share Dad's great story with them.

To my friends at HarperOne and HarperCollins Children's Books: Judith Curr, Miles Doyle, Suzanne Quist, Karen Chaplin, and everyone at Harper. Thank you for making us feel like family.

To Stanlee Stahl and the Jewish Foundation for the Righteous: Thank you for honoring Dad so richly.

To the congregations of West Haven Baptist Church, Knoxville, Tennessee, and Piney Grove Baptist Church, Maryville, Tennessee: Thank you for your endless love and ceaseless mercy.

To Dr. Chad Berry: Thank you for the history project that sparked Lauren's interest and our discovery.

Thank you to good friends: YOKE Youth Ministries, Camp BA-YO-CA, Jim Tipton, Chuck Morris, Jenny

Stansberry, Heather Hatcher, Rhonda Smithson, Chris Coyne, Eric Trager, Congressman John J. Duncan Jr., Senator Bob Corker, Senator Lamar Alexander, Governor Bill Haslam, Congressman Tim Burchett, Senator Marsha Blackburn, Howard Kohr, Robert Cohen, Brad Gordon, John and Diana Hagee, Shari Dollinger, Lyndon Allen, Jonathan Greenblatt, Ezra Friedlander, Mitchell Edmonds, Teresa Young, Mary Jean Gunden, Arie and Tammy Kraus, Arlene and Paul Samuels, Carl Wouters, Doug Mitchell, Gary and Cindy Smith, Danise Peters, Cathy Hinesley, Joel Anand Samy, Natasha Srdoc, Bill Etheridge, Paul Brothwood, Nathan Weinbaum, Charles and Joanne Teichman, Joseph Krygier, Lisa Ades, Marcy Miller, Eric Vanslander, Megan Harris, Penny Simon, Ted Koppel, Dan Moulthrop, Danielle Kahane-Kaminsky, Jim Snyder, Dr. Jerry Westbrook, Donnie and Rhonda Douglas, Rachel McRae, Preston Trotter, and many more friends too numerous to mention.

Thank you and blessings to all US veterans, the 106th Infantry "Golden Lions" Division, and the 422nd Regiment, and army captain Edward Bruce Foster Sr. of Knoxville.

Most important, God bless every American POW at Stalag IXA and especially the 255 GIs who signed Dad's journal. We salute all—all are heroes.

SELECTED REFERENCES

Ades, Lisa. *GI Jews: Jewish Americans in World War II.* Television documentary. Public Broadcasting System, 2018.

Atkinson, Rick with Kate Waters. *Battle of the Bulge: The Young Readers Adaptation.* New York: Henry Holt and Company, 2015.

Atkinson, Rick. *The Guns at Last Light: The War in Western Europe, 1944–1945, Volume Three of the Liberation Trilogy.* New York: Henry Holt and Company, 2013.

Beevor, Antony. *Ardennes 1944: The Battle of the Bulge.* New York: Penguin Books, 2015.

Caddick-Adams, Peter. *Snow and Steel: The Battle of the Bulge, 1944–45.* Oxford, UK: Oxford University Press, 2015.

Churchill, Winston S. *Triumph and Tragedy.* Boston: Houghton Mifflin Company, 1953.

Cohen, Roger. *Soldiers and Slaves: American POWs Trapped by the Nazis' Final Gamble.* New York: Alfred A. Knopf, 2005.

Cole, Hugh M. *The Ardennes: The Battle of the Bulge (US Military History of WW II Green Book)*. Washington, DC: CMH Publishing, 1965.

Collins, Michael, Ken Johnson, and Martin King. *Warriors of the 106th: The Last Infantry Division of World War II*. Philadelphia: Casemate Publishers, 2017.

Dupuy, Colonel R. Earnest. *St. Vith Lion in the Way: The 106th Division in World War II*. Washington, DC: Infantry Journal Press, 1949.

Frankl, Viktor E. *Man's Search for Meaning*. Boston: Beacon Press, 1949.

Fussel, Paul. *The Boys' Crusade: The American Infantry in Northwestern Europe, 1944–1945*. New York: Modern Library, 2003.

Guggenheim, Charles. *Berga Soldiers of Another War*. Television documentary. Public Broadcasting System, 2002.

Hilberg, Raul. *The Destruction of the European Jews*. Chicago: Quadrangle Books, 1961.

Kershaw, Alex. *The Longest Winter: The Battle of the Bulge and the Epic Story of World War II's Most Decorated Platoon*. Cambridge, MA: Da Capo Press, 2005.

Kershaw, Ian. *The End: The Defiance and Destruction of Hitler's Germany, 1944–1945*. New York: Penguin Books, 2011.

MacDonald, Charles B. *A Time for Trumpets: The Untold Story of the Battle of the Bulge*. New York: Perennial, 1997.

———. *Company Commander: The Classic Infantry Memoir of*

WWII. Ithaca, NY: Burford Books, 1947.

McManus, John C. *Alamo in the Ardennes: The Untold Story of the American Soldiers Who Made the Defense of Bastogne Possible*. Hoboken, NJ: John Wiley & Sons, 2007.

McMillin, Woody. *In the Presence of Soldiers: The 2nd Army Maneuvers & Other World War II Activity in Tennessee*. Nashville: Horton Heights Press, 2010.

Merriam, Robert E. Dark. *December: The Full Account of the Battle of the Bulge*. Chicago: Ziff-Davis, 1947.

Messenger, Charles. *Sepp Dietrich: Hitler's Gladiator*. New York: Brassey's, 1988.

Mordecai Paldiel. *The Paths of the Righteous: Gentile Rescuers of Jews During the Holocaust*. Hoboken, NJ: KTAV Publishing House, 1993.

Morse, John. *The Sitting Duck Division: Attacked from the Rear*. San Jose, CA: Writers Club Press, 2001.

Nobecourt, Jacques. *Hitler's Last Gamble: The Battle of the Ardennes* (translated from the French by R.H. Barry). London: Chatto & Windus, 1967.

Parker, Danny S. *Battle of the Bulge: Hitler's Ardennes Offensive 1944–1945*. Cambridge, MA: Da Capo Press, 2004.

Peterson, Richard. *Healing the Child Warrior: A Search for Inner Peace*. Largo, FL: CombatVets Network, 1992.

Pyle, Ernie. *Brave Men*. New York: Henry Holt and Company, 1944.

Reynolds, Michael. *Men of Steel: I SS Panzer Corps: The*

Ardennes and Eastern Front 1944–45. New York: Sarpedon, 1999.

Schrijvers, Peter. *Those Who Hold Bastogne: The True Story of the Soldiers and Civilians Who Fought in the Biggest Battle of the Bulge*. New Haven, CT: Yale University Press, 2014.

Sheaner, Herb. *Prisoner's Odyssey*. Bloomington, IN: Xlibris Corporation, 2009.

Stahl, Stanlee, and Paul Allman. *Footsteps of My Father*. West Orange, NJ: The Jewish Foundation for the Righteous, 2018.

Strawson, John. *The Battle for the Ardennes*. London: B.T. Batsford Ltd., 1972.

Toland, John. *Adolf Hitler: The Definitive Biography*. New York: Anchor Books, 1976.

Toland, John. *Battle: The Story of the Bulge*. New York: Random House, 1959.

Whitlock, Flint. *Given Up for Dead: American GIs in the Nazi Concentration Camp at Berga*. New York: Westview Press, 2005.

Wiesel, Elie. *Night*. New York: Hill and Wang, 1960.

TIMELINE OF WORLD WAR II

January 30, 1933: Adolf Hitler becomes chancellor of Germany.

March 1933: Nazis open Dachau concentration camp.

October 25, 1936: Nazi Germany and Fascist Italy sign a treaty known as the Rome-Berlin Axis treaty.

November 25, 1936: Nazi Germany and Imperial Japan sign a pact against Russia and communism.

July 7, 1937: Japan invades China.

March 12, 1938: Hitler annexes Austria into Germany.

March 15, 1938: Nazis invade Czechoslovakia.

September 1, 1939: Germany invades Poland, marking the beginning of what will become World War II.

September 3, 1939: France, Great Britain, Australia, and New Zealand declare war on Germany.

April–June 1940: Germany invades Denmark and Norway.

May–June 1940: Germany takes over the Netherlands, Belgium, and northern France.

May 10, 1940: Winston Churchill becomes prime minister of Great Britain.

June 10, 1940: Italy joins the Axis powers.

July–October 1940: Germany launches air attacks on Great Britain, known as the Battle of Britain.

September 27, 1940: Germany, Italy, and Japan create the Axis alliance.

June 22, 1941: Axis powers attack Russia with four million troops.

December 7, 1941: Japanese attack Pearl Harbor.

December 8, 1941: The United States enters World War II on the side of the Allies.

June 6, 1944: D-Day and the Normandy invasion; Allied forces invade France.

August 25, 1944: Paris is liberated from German control.

December 16, 1944: Germany launches the Battle of the Bulge.

April 12, 1945: President Franklin Roosevelt dies; Harry Truman becomes president.

April 30, 1945: Hitler commits suicide when he knows Germany has lost the war.

May 7, 1945: Germany surrenders.

August 6, 1945: The United States drops the atomic bomb on Hiroshima, Japan.

August 9, 1945: The United States drops a second atomic bomb on Nagasaki, Japan.

September 2, 1945: Japan surrenders to the United States.

FURTHER READING: WORLD WAR II BIBLIOGRAPHY

Atwood, Kathryn J. *Women Heroes of World War II: 32 Stories of Espionage, Sabotage, Resistance, and Rescue.* Chicago: Chicago Review Press, 2019.

Bearce, Stephanie. *Top Secret Files: World War II: Spies, Secret Missions, and Hidden Facts from World War II.* Waco, TX: Prufrock Press, 2014.

Bruchac, Joseph. *Code Talker: A Novel About the Navajo Marines of World War Two.* New York: Speak, 2006.

Colman, Penny. *Rosie the Riveter: Women Working on the Home Front in World War II.* New York: Yearling, 1998.

DK, *World War II: Visual Encyclopedia.* New York: DK Children, 2015.

Freedman, Russell. *We Will Not Be Silent: The White Rose Student Resistance Movement That Defied Adolf Hitler.* New York: Clarion Books, 2016.

Gratz, Alan. *Projekt 1065: A Novel of World War II.* New York: Scholastic, 2016.

Hopkinson, Deborah. *D-Day: The World War II Invasion That Changed History.* New York: Scholastic, 2018.

————. *How I Became a Spy: A Mystery of WWII London.* New York: Knopf Books for Young Readers, 2019.

Lowry, Lois. *Number the Stars,* 25th anniversary ed. New York: HMH Books for Young Readers, 2014.

Marrin, Albert. *Uprooted: The Japanese American Experience During World War II.* New York: Knopf Books for Young Readers, 2016.

Mundy, Liza. *Code Girls: The True Story of the American Women Who Secretly Broke Codes in World War II (Young Readers Edition).* New York: Little, Brown Books for Young Readers, 2018.

Murray, Doug, and Anthony Williams. *D-Day: The Liberation of Europe Begins (Graphic Battles of World War II).* New York: Rosen Central, 2008.

Nicholson, Dorinda. *Remember World War II: Kids Who Survived Tell Their Stories.* Washington, DC: National Geographic Children's Books, 2015.

Panchyk, Richard and John McCain. *World War II for Kids: A History with 21 Activities.* Chicago: Chicago Review Press, 2002.

Pearson, P. O'Connell. *Fly Girls: The Daring American Women Pilots Who Helped Win World War II.* New York: Simon & Schuster Books for Young Readers, 2018.

Raum, Elizabeth. *A World War II Timeline.* North Mankato, MN: Capstone Press, 2014.

Stelson, Caren. *Sachiko: A Nagasaki Bomb Survivor's Story.* Minneapolis, MN: Carolrhoda Books, 2016.

Zullo, Allan. *10 True Tales: World War II Heroes.* New York: Scholastic, 2015.

INDEX

Page numbers in italics refer to photographs.

AR Level _____ Lexile _____

AR Pts. _____ RC Pts._____